The Presidents' Chronicles

A Legacy of Leadership in America

Nakel W. A. Nikiema

© **Copyright 2025 - All rights reserved.**

The content contained within this book may not be reproduced, duplicated or transmitted without direct written permission from the author or the publisher.

Under no circumstances will any blame or legal responsibility be held against the publisher, or author, for any damages, reparation, or monetary loss due to the information contained within this book, either directly or indirectly.

<u>Legal Notice:</u>

This book is copyright protected. It is only for personal use. You cannot amend, distribute, sell, use, quote or paraphrase any part, or the content within this book, without the consent of the author or publisher.

<u>Disclaimer Notice:</u>

Please note the information contained within this document is for educational and entertainment purposes only. All effort has been executed to present accurate, up to date, reliable, complete information. No warranties of any kind are declared or implied. Readers acknowledge that the author is not engaged in the rendering of legal, financial, medical or professional advice. The content within this book has been derived from various sources. Please consult a licensed professional before attempting any techniques outlined in this book.

By reading this document, the reader agrees that under no circumstances is the author responsible for any losses, direct or indirect, that are incurred as a result of the use of the information contained within this document, including, but not limited to, errors, omissions, or inaccuracies.

Table of Contents

INTRODUCTION 1

CHAPTER 1 THE FOUNDATION OF LEADERSHIP 5

   WASHINGTON'S PRESIDENTIAL PRECEDENTS 6
      Establishment of the Presidential Cabinet 6
      Voluntary Two-Term Limit 7
      Neutrality in Foreign Conflicts 7
      Warnings in the Farewell Address 8
      Concrete Examples of Governance Frameworks 8
      Legacy of Neutrality 9
      An Enduring Legacy 9
   JOHN ADAMS'S LEGISLATION 10
      The Alien Acts 10
      The Sedition Act and Its Controversy 10
      Opposition and the Virginia and Kentucky Resolutions 11
      Broader Implications and Legacy 12
   JEFFERSON'S RESPONSE AND THE LOUISIANA PURCHASE 12
      Strategic Importance of the Louisiana Territory 13
      Negotiations and the Constitutional Debate 14
      Strict vs. Broad Constitutional Interpretation 14
      Implications for Native American Sovereignty 15
      Economic Advancements 15
      The Evolution of Governance and Executive Power 16
   MADISON'S LEADERSHIP DURING THE WAR OF 1812 16
      Madison's Governance and the War as a Central Event 17
      Declaration of War and Executive Power 17
      Challenges and Resilience 18
      Nationalism and the Treaty of Ghent 18
      Balancing State and Federal Powers 19
      Foreign Policy and National Identity 19
      The Era of Good Feelings 20
      Leadership and Governance in Times of Trial 20
   CONCLUDING THOUGHTS 21

CHAPTER 2 NATIONAL UNITY AND DIVISION 23

THE MONROE DOCTRINE'S IMPACT ON FOREIGN POLICY 24
    Declaration of American Dominance.. 24
    European Reactions.. 24
JACKSON'S INDIAN REMOVAL ACT AND ITS CONSEQUENCES 25
    Opposition and Legal Resistance.. 26
    Legacy and Transition to Lincoln's Leadership................................ 27
LINCOLN AND THE PRESERVATION OF THE UNION 27
    Lincoln's Vision of Unity.. 28
    Balancing Firmness and Empathy.. 28
    Redefining the War's Purpose.. 29
    Opposition and Division... 29
    Legacy of Unity and Reconstruction.. 30
ANDREW JOHNSON'S STRUGGLES DURING RECONSTRUCTION........................... 31
    Johnson's Approach to Reconstruction....................................... 31
    Legislative Battles and Power Struggles..................................... 32
    Leniency Toward the South and Black Codes.................................. 32
    Resistance to Black Empowerment Movements.................................. 33
    Historians' Perspectives of Johnson... 33
    Lessons From Johnson's Presidency... 34
CONCLUDING THOUGHTS... 35

CHAPTER 3 PRESIDENTIAL RESPONSES TO INDUSTRIAL GROWTH AND SOCIAL CHANGE 37

PRESIDENT THEODORE ROOSEVELT: A LEADER OF CHANGE 38
    Presidency and Progressive Reforms.. 38
    Trust-Busting Efforts... 38
TAFT'S APPROACH TO TRUST-BUSTING.. 39
    Taft's Inclusive Approach to Antitrust...................................... 40
    The Payne-Aldrich Tariff.. 40
    Public Perception and Challenges.. 41
    Contributions to Antitrust Enforcement...................................... 41
    Contradictions in Leadership.. 42
    The Dual Legacy of Taft's Presidency.. 42
    Intensified Antitrust Efforts... 43
    Political Struggles and Internal Discord.................................... 43
    The Legacy of Antitrust Enforcement... 44
WILSON AND THE PROGRESSIVE ERA REFORMS..................................... 45
    Wilson's New Freedom Program.. 45
    Federal Trade Commission.. 46

    The Clayton Antitrust Act *46*
    Economic and Social Reforms *47*
    Impact and Challenges *47*
    The Federal Reserve Act *48*
    The Legacy of Wilson's New Freedom Program *48*
  THE FEDERAL RESERVE ACT'S IMPACT 49
    A Flexible and Sturdy Banking Framework *49*
    Instilling Public Confidence *50*
    Economic Cooperation and Planning *50*
    The Great Depression and Subsequent Reforms *51*
    World War II and the Treasury Accord *51*
    Contemporary Relevance *52*
    The Progressive Era's Foundations *52*
  CONCLUDING THOUGHTS 53

CHAPTER 4 DEPRESSION, WAR, AND RECOVERY **55**

  FDR'S NEW DEAL AND INFRASTRUCTURE REFORMS 56
    The First 100 Days *56*
    The Social Security Act and Addressing Financial Instability *57*
    Agricultural Reforms *57*
    Uneven Distribution of Benefits *58*
    Legacy of the New Deal *58*
  A HIGHWAY SYSTEM AND ECONOMIC TRANSFORMATION 59
    Suburbanization and Cultural Shifts *60*
    Economic Value and Job Creation *60*
    Strategic Military Importance *61*
    Revitalizing Cities and Logistics Innovations *61*
    Social Implications *62*
    Cold War Preparedness and Multifunctional Infrastructure *62*
    Transition to the New Frontier *63*
    Roads as Conduits for Change *63*
  INFRASTRUCTURE AND SOCIAL CHANGES 63
    The Space Race and Technological Advancements *64*
    Educational Investments and Societal Growth *65*
    The Civil Rights Movement and Legislative Action *65*
    Economic Opportunity and Global Leadership *66*
    Legacy of Innovation and Equality *66*
    Patterns of Leadership and Societal Impact *66*
    The Power of Investment *67*
    Visionary Leadership and Long-Term Impacts *67*
  CONCLUDING THOUGHTS 68

CHAPTER 5 CIVIL RIGHTS LEADERSHIP 71

LBJ'S CIVIL RIGHTS ACT AND GREAT SOCIETY 72
- *The Great Society Program.. 72*
- *Criticism and Impact.. 73*
- *A Complicated Legacy 74*
- *Reshaping the Civil Rights Dialogue 74*

NIXON'S AND FORD'S POLICIES 75
- *Nixon's Busing Policy 75*
- *Ford's Civil Rights Policies 76*
- *Affirmative Action and Representation 76*
- *The Nixon Pardon 76*
- *Shifting Republican Attitudes Toward Equality 77*
- *A Commitment to Human Rights.. 77*
- *Ford's Role in Shaping Civil Rights 78*
- *Bridging Civil Rights Efforts 78*
- *Carter's Human Rights Advocacy 79*
- *Intertwining Foreign and Domestic Policy.................................. 80*
- *Strategic Use of Human Rights... 80*
- *Expanding Civil Rights at Home 81*
- *Grassroots Movements and Global Advocacy 81*
- *Public Awareness and Modern Governance 81*
- *A Blueprint for Fairness and Justice.. 82*
- *A Legacy of Inclusive Governance 83*

CONCLUDING THOUGHTS... 83

CHAPTER 6 COLD WAR CHALLENGES 85

COLD WAR STRATEGIES AND MILITARY INITIATIVES 86
- *Public and Political Discourse 86*
- *Financial Prioritization and Economic Impact 87*
- *Diplomatic Engagement and Arms Reduction............................ 87*
- *The Cultural Impact of the Arms Race 88*
- *Legacy and Influence on Geopolitical Dynamics......................... 88*
- *Reshaping Cold War Politics 89*

TRANSFORMATION IN GEOPOLITICAL ALLIANCES.. 89
- *NATO Enlargement and Collective Security................................ 90*
- *Diplomacy and Democratic Engagement 90*
- *NATO Expansion as a Strategic Tool... 91*
- *Military Interventions in the Balkans.. 91*
- *Controversies and Challenges 92*
- *Globalization and Trade Policies 93*

Legacy of Clinton's Foreign Policy.. 93
END OF THE COLD WAR AND BROADER IMPLICATIONS................................. 93
  Beyond the Iron Curtain... 94
  Foundations in Cold War Strategies 94
  Kennedy's Diplomatic Balancing Act 95
  Nixon's Pragmatic Diplomacy.. 95
  Carter's Human Rights Emphasis.. 96
  Reagan's Technological and Economic Strategy 96
  Post–Cold War Realities.. 96
  Legacy of Cold War Strategies... 97
  Bridging Historical Precedents With Modern Challenges 98
CONCLUDING THOUGHTS.. 98

CHAPTER 7 CONTEMPORARY IDEOLOGICAL SHIFTS 99

GEORGE W. BUSH'S WAR ON TERROR 100
  Counterterrorism and Civil Liberties 100
  Economic Anxiety.. 101
  Populism and Party Realignments... 101
  Liberalism and Government Power 102
  National Security vs. Democratic Principles............................. 102
  Bipartisanship and Polarization... 103
  Policy Examples and Public Discourse..................................... 103
  Domestic Policy Priorities 104
OBAMA'S AFFORDABLE CARE ACT 104
  Universal Health Coverage 105
  The Government's Role in Health Care 105
  Partisan Tensions and Doctrinal Conflict................................. 106
  Grassroots Movements and Health Care Advocacy................... 106
  Legacy and Social Welfare Precedents 106
  Misinformation and Political Rhetoric..................................... 107
  Broader Implications for Social Safety Nets............................. 107
  Modern Conservatism 108
TRUMP'S ECONOMIC POLICIES AND TRADE WARS 108
  Protectionism and Redefining Conservatism............................ 109
  Impact on Rural and Working-Class Voters.............................. 109
  Divides in the Republican Party.. 110
  Legacy of Trade Wars 110
  Globalization and Economic Sovereignty................................. 111
  National Rhetoric and Cultural Identity................................... 111
  Intersectionality of Economic Policy 111
  Debates on Economic Nationalism and Interventionism............ 112

    Environmental Policies 112
    Legacy of Economic Nationalism 113
  SHIFTS IN ENVIRONMENTAL POLICIES 113
    Deregulation and Market-Oriented Environmentalism 114
    Regulatory vs. Market-Based Approaches 114
    Climate Adaptation and Resilience 115
    Grassroots Movements and Advocacy 115
    Youth Activism and Normative Shifts 116
    Legislative Examples and Conceptual Divides 116
    Science, Policy, and Public Perception 117
    Electoral Politics and Environmental Advocacy 117
  CONCLUDING THOUGHTS 118

CHAPTER 8 INFLUENCE OF PUBLIC OPINION IN LEADERSHIP 119

  THE INFLUENCE OF PUBLIC COMMUNICATION STRATEGIES 120
    Bridging Policy and Personal Outreach 120
    The New Deal and Public Reassurance 121
    Codes of Fair Practice 121
    Building Trust and Leadership Confidence 122
    The Legacy of the Fireside Chats 122
    Communication Strategies Across Eras 122
  NAVIGATING PROTESTS AND PUBLIC DISSENT 123
    Reluctance to Engage Public Sentiment 123
    The Impact of Anti-War Protests 124
    Vietnamization: A Strategic Concession 124
    The Pentagon Papers and Public Mistrust 124
    Balancing Domestic Unrest and Foreign Policy 125
    Reactive Governance and Public Influence 126
    Clinton's Communication Strategy 126
  SCANDAL MANAGEMENT AND MODERN MEDIA ENGAGEMENT 127
    Clinton's Engagement Through Cable News and Digital Platforms 127
    Obama's Digital Revolution 128
    The Evolution of Media and Public Engagement 128
    Scandals and Strategic Communication 129
    The Impact of Scandals on Communication Strategies 129
    Public Opinion's Role in Leadership 130
  CONCLUDING THOUGHTS 131

CHAPTER 9 THE ROLE OF PERSONAL BELIEFS 133

  JEFFERSON AND THE SEPARATION OF CHURCH AND STATE 134

- *The Virginia Statute for Religious Freedom* 134
- *Challenges and Controversies* 135
- *Jefferson's Writings and Vision for Secularism* 135
- *Long-Term Implications* 136
- *Lincoln's Evolving Views* 136
- PRESIDENTS' PERSONAL VIEWS 137
  - *Lincoln's Personal Views on Emancipation* 137
- CARTER'S EMPHASIS ON MORAL LEADERSHIP 138
  - *Religious Upbringing and Integrity* 138
  - *Leading With Conviction* 138
  - *Challenges of Moral Leadership* 139
  - *Contrasts Between Lincoln and Carter* 139
  - *Carter's Legacy and Reagan's Conservative Revolution* 140
  - *Human Rights as a Foreign Policy Tenet* 140
  - *The Camp David Accords* 141
  - *Domestic Policies Rooted in Ethics* 141
  - *Addressing Social Inequities* 142
  - *Post-Presidential Legacy* 142
  - *The Power of Personal Convictions* 143
- REAGAN'S CONSERVATIVE REVOLUTION 143
  - *Economic Philosophy and Reaganomics* 144
  - *Debates and Outcomes of Fiscal Policies* 144
  - *Cold War Ideology and Military Stance* 145
  - *Diplomatic Engagement and Disarmament* 145
  - *Redefining Conservative Politics* 146
  - *Legacy of Ideological Commitment* 146
- CONCLUDING THOUGHTS 147

CHAPTER 10 PRESIDENTIAL LEGACIES AND LESSONS 149

- UNINTENDED CONSEQUENCES AND RHETORIC INFLUENCE ON DECISIONS 150
  - *War Decisions and Long-Term Effects* 150
  - *Economic Measures and Systemic Challenges* 151
  - *Social Interventions and Community Divides* 151
  - *Communication's Far-Reaching Influence* 152
  - *Expansion of Executive Power* 152
- THE EVOLUTION OF THE EXECUTIVE OFFICE AND HISTORICAL INTERPRETATION .. 153
  - *Shaping Presidential Power Through Constitutional Changes* 153
  - *Expansion of Presidential Authority* 154
  - *Public Expectations and Media Influence* 154
  - *The Presidency in a Global Context* 155
  - *Melding Domestic and Global Expectations* 156

    Rhetoric and Public Memory Influences on Legacy 156
        Messaging During National Crises.. 157
        Campaign Discourse and Public Expectations 157
        Communication and Public Trust.. 158
        Social Media's Role in Presidential Communication.................... 158
        Historiography and Evolving Narratives....................................... 159
        Cultural Manifestations of Presidential Legacies 159
        Educational Framing 160
        Shaping Legacies 160
    Concluding Thoughts.. 161

CONCLUSION...**163**

REFERENCES..**167**

Introduction

What drives someone to consider seeking the highest office in the land? Is it the allure of power, a sense of duty to their fellow citizens, or perhaps the hope of leaving a legacy that will shape history? The pursuit of the presidency is not just a journey for leaders; it's also a meaningful venture that calls out to each of us in our quest to make a difference.

Being president is a role rife with responsibility and scrutiny, where every decision has the potential to influence millions, defining the course of a nation for generations to come. This book explores the fascinating narratives of U.S. presidents, investigating their ambitions, challenges, and the indelible marks they have left on America and the world.

Anyone interested in the relationship between politics and society must understand the histories and impacts of U.S. presidents. As we look at the modern political landscape, reflecting on the choices made by past presidents can offer invaluable insights into the complexities of governance and the moral dilemmas leaders often face. Historical decisions resonate through time, providing lessons that inform us today.

Introduction

From foundational precedents set by George Washington to the multifaceted legacies of modern presidents, each administration teaches us something unique about leadership and its consequences.

Consider the evolution of domestic policies and foreign affairs that have been shaped by presidential actions. Whether it's economic reforms, civil rights advancements, or international diplomacy, these decisions highlight the far-reaching impacts of leadership. By examining the successes and failures of those who have held the highest office, we gain perspective on how history informs the present and future—a vital understanding for educators, students, and history enthusiasts alike.

This book thoroughly explores presidential history by focusing on significant moments that defined particular eras in American leadership. We begin with Washington's establishment of the presidency's boundaries and responsibilities, followed by Lincoln's resolute stance during the Civil War, Roosevelt's New Deal response to economic turmoil, and so forth, culminating in contemporary presidencies grappling with global challenges in an interconnected world.

Through this chronological examination, we will experience the evolution of presidential roles and their perennial effects on society.

In our examination, we also emphasize the importance of varied perspectives. Leadership is about the decisions made at the top and how those decisions reverberate through every part of society. To truly grasp American history, we must listen to the voices often left unheard—those who lived under the influence of presidential decisions, whether in support or opposition. Including these varied viewpoints refines our narrative, offering a more nuanced understanding of how leadership shapes lives and communities.

For educators and students engaged in history and social studies, this text supports the development of critical-thinking skills by encouraging discussions about presidential leadership and governance. Meanwhile, general readers looking to engage in narratives will find accessible accounts connecting past presidential actions with contemporary issues. These stories deepen one's understanding of how historical leadership impacts today's society, encouraging an appreciation for the enduring influence of the presidency.

Through an objective lens, narrative writing is used to transform historical facts into compelling stories. You'll find simple, modern language to ensure that the content remains approachable while maintaining an engaging and consistent tone throughout. My goal is to captivate you, the reader, guiding you through the deep layers of presidential history while providing valuable insights and perspectives.

As we investigate U.S. presidential history, prepare to be captivated by the powerful narratives that reveal the essence of leadership. The stories of past presidents highlight the journey of triumphs and trials, guiding us forward and teaching us valuable lessons in courage, vision, and resilience.

In understanding their legacies, we are better equipped to face the future challenges of governance and society. Let's walk through time, where the lasting effects of our presidents still influence our lives today.

Introduction

Chapter 1

The Foundation of Leadership

In the moonlit chambers of Mount Vernon, President George Washington sat at his desk, contemplating the immense responsibility of being the newly appointed president of a nascent nation. His early decisions were not just administrative; they also established the foundation for a governing system balancing power and freedom amid revolutionary chaos.

Washington's vision required navigating unknown territory, where each choice set lasting precedents. From forming a diverse cabinet to defining executive restraint, he shaped future governance. His foundational moves aimed to ensure the fledgling republic could withstand transitions of power, underscoring why the choices of America's first leader remain relevant in contemporary governance.

Chapter 1 The Foundation of Leadership

Washington's Presidential Precedents

Washington's leadership laid the foundation for American governance, with practices that continue to guide presidential duties and shape the nation's politics. As the first president, Washington understood the gravity of his position and used it to set long-lasting precedents.

His presidency established precedents that shaped American governance and political culture. His desire to collaborate with the presidential cabinet, voluntary two-term limit, commitment to neutrality, and insightful warnings in his farewell address created a framework for future leaders. These principles encouraged effective governance and emphasized the importance of national unity.

Establishment of the Presidential Cabinet

Collaborative governance began with the formation of the presidential cabinet, prioritizing multiple perspectives in decision-making. Washington surrounded himself with knowledgeable advisors, creating an administrative structure that future presidents would emulate for more informed governance.

The presidential cabinet introduced collective leadership, drawing on various viewpoints. The initial cabinet included the departments of State, Treasury, and War, along with the attorney general, guiding national decisions through collective wisdom.

This model emphasized inclusivity, allowing diverse opinions to inform critical choices. Washington's actions highlighted the importance of building a team of experts, showing that a leader's strength lies in the wisdom they garner from others. This laid a foundation for future cabinet work and collaborative practices across all levels of government (Greenspan, 2025).

Voluntary Two-Term Limit

Washington's decision to voluntarily step down after two terms in office was another monumental precedent. In deciding against running for a third term, he reframed leadership as a temporary service, emphasizing the value of peaceful power transfer. This set a new norm that was not legally binding but shaped the U.S. presidential structure until Franklin D. Roosevelt broke it in 1940 (NCC Staff, 2020).

His example emphasized the democratic principle that no one individual should hold too much power for too long. This voluntary relinquishment of authority signified strength and integrity in leadership, embedding the idea that leaders should serve the nation's interest over personal ambition (*The 2020-21 Presidential Transition*, 2022).

Neutrality in Foreign Conflicts

Washington's stance on neutrality in foreign conflicts further established lasting diplomatic precedents. By choosing this path, he prioritized national interests and set a standard of non-involvement in European wars. This neutrality allowed the young nation to develop its economy and governance without the distraction or expense of foreign wars.

His decision not to involve the US in the alliances and conflicts of foreign nations was a foresight that granted flexibility in foreign policy decisions, a practice adopted by successors who sought to focus on domestic development over international crusades. His approach provided a buffer for America to grow its identity and stability on its terms, demonstrating the long-term advantage of such foresight.

Warnings in the Farewell Address

Washington's farewell address also delivered warnings against political factions and foreign alliances, highlighting the importance of unity in governance. He cautioned that political parties could lead to divisions that might jeopardize national cohesion and warned of the dangers that foreign entanglements posed to domestic tranquility (Pruitt, 2025).

These warnings remain deeply relevant today, reflecting ongoing concerns about division and allegiance. Washington's insights encouraged a steady focus on national unity and caution over foreign influences, principles at the core of maintaining stable governance.

Concrete Examples of Governance Frameworks

Washington's decisions illustrate how these approaches contributed to lasting effects on governance. His two-term precedent and emphasis on neutrality in foreign affairs remain guiding principles. The significance of mixed perspectives in decision-making through his cabinet laid a foundation for informed policy development.

This created an expectation for future administrations to consult wide-ranging views, enhancing political efficacy and ensuring that governance reflected a broad spectrum of insights.

Legacy of Neutrality

Washington's insistence on neutrality shaped foreign policy attitudes and inspired a tradition of prioritizing internal affairs while cautiously approaching international engagement. This focus on non-intervention assured that policies agreed with American interests, preserving independence in foreign strategy. The long-term implications of such neutrality granted succeeding presidents a platform prioritizing American growth and stability over external entanglements (Chervinsky, 2025).

An Enduring Legacy

With these precedents, Washington's role transcended his immediate policy impact, building and leaving a legacy focused on sustainable governance practices. His farewell address's reflections on political unity and division highlighted a recognition of governance challenges that outlasted his era, reinforcing the balance needed between national interests and political dynamics.

His wisdom can be felt through these words: "You have in a common cause fought and triumphed together. The independence and liberty you possess are the work of joint councils and joint efforts, of common dangers, sufferings, and successes" (Washington, 1796). This relevance in today's political climate illustrates the weight of foundational leadership insights in sustaining cohesive governance.

Chapter 1 The Foundation of Leadership

John Adams's Legislation

The transition to the next administration illustrated Washington's ideals and the evolution of executive power. His precedents supported future governance as new challenges arose. President John Adams's controversial legislation highlights the complexities of executive power in early American history.

The Federalists, keenly alert to what they perceived as threats from European powers, and particularly wary of France, pushed through the Alien and Sedition Acts of 1798 during Adams's presidency. These acts allowed the government to circumvent previously held norms about immigration and expression.

The Alien Acts

The Alien Acts targeted noncitizens, most notably those from France and Ireland, whom Federalists suspected of lingering allegiances to their homelands. Federalists worried these immigrants might incite hostilities against Britain, a rival of France, consequently posing a security risk. By sharply raising residency requirements for citizenship and giving the president sweeping powers to expel foreigners, these acts imposed rigorous control designed to improve national security (*Alien and Sedition Acts (1798)*, 2023).

The Sedition Act and Its Controversy

This move stirred the pot, as many saw this legislation as extending executive power beyond acceptable limits. The fear of invasion was palpable, and Adams, after much cajoling by his party and even his wife, endorsed these acts. His signature on the Sedition Act, in particular, was controversial.

This law criminalized criticism of the government, setting off an intense debate over the balance between governance and free speech. It aimed to quash dissent from the Jeffersonian-Republicans, whose criticisms were seen as dangerous disloyalty, and led to several prosecutions, marking a stark departure from the American tradition of open debate.

The Sedition Act's impact on political dissent was deep-rooted. Newspapers critical of the government found themselves targeted, leading to a fierce standoff between Federalist ideals and the Jeffersonian-Republican press. The most notorious case was that of Luther Baldwin, whose drunken comment about a presidential salute led to legal consequences under the Sedition Act. Such prosecutions were stark illustrations of the political climate and signaled the divide on political freedoms (Leibiger, 2020).

Opposition and the Virginia and Kentucky Resolutions

Critics saw these acts as a betrayal of fundamental rights, leading Jefferson and Madison to pen the Virginia and Kentucky Resolutions in protest. While Jefferson's more drastic call for nullification flouted the Constitution's supremacy clause, both resolutions signaled a strong disagreement with broad federal overreach.

The backlash was a catalyst in the changing political tide, demonstrated by Jefferson's eventual electoral victory. Once in power, he pardoned those who had been swept up in the Sedition Act's net, yet his own administration wasn't free of contradictions. Jefferson soon adopted similarly suppressive measures against his Federalist rivals, a testament to the lingering partisan battle (The Editors of Encyclopaedia Britannica, 2020b).

Broader Implications and Legacy

The acts had significant implications beyond their political context, raising essential questions about executive and Congressional power that would continue throughout American history. While ostensibly focused on security, they seemed to be aimed more at consolidating political power and silencing opposition, creating a complicated legacy in which security and liberty clashed.

Loyalty was redefined, implying that criticism was disloyal, and the political landscape embraced binary distinctions of friend and enemy. Amid rising partisan extremism, Adams's actions—driven by longstanding party loyalty—appeared as both defense mechanisms and troubling precursors to potential authoritarian governance.

Jefferson's Response and the Louisiana Purchase

As we'll explore in this section, President Thomas Jefferson's decisions, especially the Louisiana Purchase, were reactions against Adams's precedents. He aimed to unify executive power, diminishing divisiveness while undermining the Federalists. Aware of Adams's political fallout, he adopted a conciliatory approach to governance and expanded American territory.

In essence, these acts demonstrate how leaders operate under perceived threats and pressures, an insight that remains relevant today. They force an examination of the perennial balancing act between safeguarding a nation and protecting the freedoms upon which it is built—an issue as relevant today as it was in 1798. With great awareness of these balance-of-power dynamics, future administrations could glean much from these past actions and their substantial legacies.

In the wake of Adams's controversial Alien and Sedition Acts, which challenged civil liberties and expanded executive powers, Jefferson's handling of federal authority during the Louisiana Purchase offers a poignant illustration of early presidential leadership grappling with constitutional boundaries.

Let's investigate Jefferson's seminal decision to acquire the Louisiana Territory, a move that reshaped the nation and forced Jefferson to reconsider the scope of federal power. The purchase, occurring through pragmatic yet constitutionally uncertain negotiations, marked a critical step in the young nation's territorial and ideological expansion, personifying the burgeoning concept of Manifest Destiny that would define American foreign policy and westward movement for decades to come.

Manifest Destiny, a term first used in 1845, refers to the belief that the United States was divinely chosen to expand its territory, promoting democracy and capitalism throughout North America (History.com Editors, 2025h).

Strategic Importance of the Louisiana Territory

Thomas Jefferson, aware of the Louisiana Territory's strategic importance, faced a dilemma when the region shifted from Spanish to French control. France, under Napoleon Bonaparte, posed a more formidable challenge than Spain, mainly due to its military prowess and expansive ambitions. The Mississippi River, vital for American trade and economic growth, transformed the acquisition of New Orleans and adjacent lands from a strategic interest into an economic necessity.

Jefferson's previously friendly relations with France complicated the matter, as diplomatic tensions now arose over territorial control. This concern became evident as reports confirmed France's regained authority over Louisiana, pressuring the United States to secure access to the Mississippi River as a commercial lifeline (Casper, 2022).

Negotiations and the Constitutional Debate

Confronted with the possibility of French hostility disrupting American trade, Jefferson strategically negotiated the acquisition of New Orleans. Initially, he offered to purchase the city and West Florida. To Jefferson's surprise, France counter-offered the entire Louisiana Territory for $15 million, an opportunity made urgent by Napoleon's need to fund military campaigns in Europe.

Recognizing the enormous potential of this "noble bargain," Jefferson accepted, despite doubts about the constitutionality of such a purchase. The Constitution did not explicitly grant the president authority to acquire new land through purchase, sparking heated debate over presidential powers (Lewis, 2020).

Strict vs. Broad Constitutional Interpretation

This acquisition forced Jefferson to weigh a strict-versus-broad constitutional interpretation. He ultimately sided with a pragmatic approach, enacting the purchase based on the broader national interest—a viewpoint that set a precedent for future executive decisions. The Louisiana Purchase legally expanded the United States, doubling its size and providing a substantial landmass imperative for agrarian development.

On top of that, this monumental decision also stressed the notion of Manifest Destiny, invigorating American aspirations to spread westward across the continent and cementing the economic and political implications of such expansion (NCC Staff, 2023).

Implications for Native American Sovereignty

Yet, Jefferson's purchase carried notable complications. It intensified debates about Native American sovereignty and their lands, as the United States asserted control over territories inhabited by diversified Indigenous communities. The newly acquired land increased government responsibility for negotiations with Native tribes, emphasizing sovereignty conflicts and introducing intricacies regarding Indigenous autonomy.

This element of expansionism laid bare the tensions between American growth and existing Indigenous rights, challenges that persisted in subsequent policies as settlers encroached westward (The Editors of Encyclopaedia Britannica, 2025a).

Economic Advancements

Economically, the Louisiana Purchase spurred agricultural and commercial advances. The acquisition facilitated trade by securing critical access routes, catalyzing American economic development. The newly gained lands contributed to a boom in agriculture, boosting the nation's position as a producer of raw goods and setting the stage for increased exports.

Jefferson envisioned an agrarian society thriving across the newly expanded nation, a dream that pushed American settlement and cultivation forward, reinforcing land as a measure of wealth and national prosperity (Casper, 2022).

The Evolution of Governance and Executive Power

Throughout this transformative period, Jefferson's handling of the constitutional and diplomatic implications of the purchase spotlighted the evolution of American governance. By successfully expanding the country and leading a new United States, Jefferson influenced the presidency's role in foreign affairs, demonstrating a flexible yet decisive use of executive power.

This pragmatic approach to leadership would echo in future administrations, shaping discussions on the balance between federal authority and constitutional adherence in environmental, territorial, and international policies. The Louisiana Purchase represents the bulk of Jefferson's legacy, reflecting early American governance's adaptability amid continental expansion.

Madison's Leadership During the War of 1812

The challenges of the Louisiana Purchase didn't end with Jefferson's presidency. It influenced James Madison's administration, as well. Madison dealt with territorial expansion, wartime governance, and pressures from previous expansionist strategies compounded by international conflicts. This contrasted Jefferson's diplomatic growth approach, emphasizing a thematic shift toward preservation and conflict resolution in presidential leadership.

Jefferson's bold approach to territorial expansion, while confronting issues of constitutional interpretation, set a backdrop for the complexities Madison would encounter. While only the third and fourth presidents, these issues were new to both men and the US and had to be laid out carefully and logically. The decisions they made during this period have remained part of the country's federal authority and foreign policy—even now, more than 200 years later.

Madison's Governance and the War as a Central Event

Madison, often heralded as the "Father of the Constitution," brought his deep understanding of governance into his presidency, a period marked by external threats and the internal task of nation-building. The War of 1812, a central event during Madison's leadership, was fueled by British trade restrictions and the abduction of American sailors.

These violations of neutrality tested Madison's capacity to balance diplomatic resolution and assertive actions. He faced increasing pressure to defend the nation's sovereignty, a struggle that mirrored the dilemmas Jefferson encountered with European powers regarding territorial claims (Reeder, 2024).

Declaration of War and Executive Power

The declaration of war against Britain in 1812 demonstrated Madison's willingness to step into conflict when diplomacy fell short. This decision demonstrated the evolving nature of executive power as Madison called upon his deep constitutional knowledge to justify military engagement.

Yet, his leadership was not without adversity. The young nation's resources and military were strained under the war's demands, crystallizing the challenges of sustaining a protracted conflict.

Challenges and Resilience

Throughout the War of 1812, Madison's government faced significant setbacks, including the burning of Washington, DC. These events deeply tested national resilience but also ignited a sense of unity. Victories, such as the Battle of New Orleans, which occurred after the war's technical conclusion, boosted national morale and reflected Madison's ability to inspire despite great adversity.

The victories and losses alike highlighted Madison's working through the limits and extensions of executive power. His administration worked tirelessly to ensure that the republic withstood threats to its sovereignty, reinforcing the authority and responsibility vested in the presidential office (*The Presidency of James Madison*, 2023).

Nationalism and the Treaty of Ghent

Madison's era witnessed the crystallization of American nationalism, particularly in the war's aftermath. The resolution through the Treaty of Ghent, which significantly restored relations with Britain to pre-war status, symbolized a diplomatic success and reinforced the nascent nation's standing on the international stage.

It also cemented a newfound confidence and pride across the United States, paving the way for the "Era of Good Feelings." During this era, a spirit of political harmony briefly prevailed, in part due to the dissolution of the Federalist Party, which had opposed the war effort (The Editors of Encyclopedia Britannica, 2024b).

Balancing State and Federal Powers

Domestically, Madison's leadership had lasting consequences for American governance, just as Jefferson's did. His decisions during wartime emphasized the importance of balancing state and federal powers. This balance, foundational to his vision of a functioning republic, influenced subsequent presidents as they, too, faced the challenges of leading a complex federal system through periods of turmoil and peace.

Madison's handling of issues such as internal improvements, as illustrated by his veto of the Bonus Bill of 1817, highlighted his strict constitutional interpretations, which nonetheless left room for debate about federal authority.

Foreign Policy and National Identity

Madison's presidency also set a precedent for how the United States approached foreign policy, blending principle with pragmatic action. His tenure demonstrated an American commitment to sovereignty and self-definition, major components of the expanding national identity.

By engaging in war, his administration stimulated a culture of resilience and adaptation that would persist throughout American history, echoing in future diplomatic and military policy decisions.

Chapter 1 The Foundation of Leadership

The Era of Good Feelings

The "Era of Good Feelings" that followed Madison's presidency was more than a time of political calm; it represented an acknowledgment of the united front the US displayed when up against adversity. Although sectional tensions simmered below the surface, the temporary lull offered a space for national reflection and growth.

The period saw infrastructural and economic development influenced by the national pride and unity crystallized during Madison's administration, influencing legislative priorities and public policies well into the future (The Editors of Encyclopaedia Britannica, 2024b).

Madison's contributions to American governance extended beyond the immediate context of his presidency, with effects rippling into the nation's approach to leadership and international relations. He built on Jefferson's foundation of expansiveness—not just of territory, but of American ideals, too—with a commitment to a republic resilient against internal divisions and external threats.

Leadership and Governance in Times of Trial

Through the lens of Madison's leadership, one witnesses the early presidency's dynamic interplay between expanding authority and retaining democratic principles. This balance, though fraught with tension and challenge, underscored the evolving nature of American governance. As the nation matured beyond these formative years, Madison's example informed future leaders who would face their unique tests with the same foundational principles of liberty and the indomitable American spirit.

This analysis of his presidency illustrates the lasting impact of Madison's decisions on national identity, demonstrating how leadership can redefine governance during times of trial. By piloting through war and peace, Madison left an indelible mark on America's political system, influencing his immediate successors and the broader trajectory of U.S. history as it moved forward from these early developmental years.

Concluding Thoughts

Washington's presidency set critical precedents that shaped American governance, establishing key principles that influenced future leaders. John Adams's administration faced complexities, particularly through the controversial Alien and Sedition Acts, challenging civil liberties and expanding executive power. Thomas Jefferson responded by acquiring the Louisiana Territory, carefully handling constitutional boundaries while expanding the nation and embracing the notion of Manifest Destiny.

Lastly, James Madison's tenure during the War of 1812 showed the evolving nature of presidential authority, balancing national security and diplomatic resolution. Collectively, these presidents built a legacy of governance characterized by strength, adaptation, and a commitment to foundational democratic principles.

In the next chapter, we'll look at how presidencies uniquely shaped national identity and sectional divides, highlighting the Monroe Doctrine's defining influence on American foreign policy and Johnson's Reconstruction challenges.

Chapter 1 The Foundation of Leadership

Chapter 2

National Unity and Division

In the early 19th century, the United States aimed to assert its voice on the world stage in an era of powerful European empires. President James Monroe declared that any European encroachment on American soil would be viewed as an affront to U.S. sovereignty, forming the basis of the Monroe Doctrine, a bold assertion of America's confidence in international affairs.

However, internally, America faced division as President Andrew Jackson's Indian Removal Act forced thousands of Native Americans from their lands, exposing the gap between national ideals and the realities of marginalized communities. This era illustrates how leadership shapes national identity and reveals tensions between unity and division.

In this chapter, we'll investigate the Monroe Doctrine, which asserted American dominance in the Western Hemisphere, shaping foreign policy to deter European interference. This shift laid the groundwork for examining domestic issues, particularly the Indian Removal Act, which reflected America's complex and often contradictory ideals during expansion.

The Monroe Doctrine's Impact on Foreign Policy

The Monroe Doctrine, articulated by James Monroe in 1823, marked an important shift in American foreign policy. Originating from the concern over European intervention in Latin America, it proclaimed that any efforts by European nations to colonize or interfere in the Americas would be viewed as acts of aggression, warranting U.S. intervention. This doctrine underscored America's growing confidence and assertiveness on the global stage, signaling a departure from its previously isolated stance.

Declaration of American Dominance

By establishing the Western Hemisphere as a sphere of influence free from European powers, the Monroe Doctrine was a bold declaration of American political and ideological dominance in the region. This policy also advanced U.S. leadership in Latin America, advocating for independence movements and encouraging positive relationships with new republics, which strengthened America's credibility as a burgeoning power (*The Monroe Doctrine*, 2022).

European Reactions

The doctrine drew mixed reactions from European powers, ranging from irritation to cautious acceptance. While some

European nations viewed it as an audacious overreach by a relatively young nation, others saw it as a practical constraint that preserved their interests without direct confrontation. The British, for instance, showed tacit support due to shared interests in maintaining open trade routes and checking rivals.

For that reason, the Monroe Doctrine significantly influenced international diplomacy by establishing a precedent for U.S. engagement in global affairs and setting a foreign policy principle that stayed in effect beyond the 19th century (Adriaenssens, 2018).

Jackson's Indian Removal Act and Its Consequences

Domestically, the Indian Removal Act of 1830 under President Andrew Jackson manifested a stark reflection of societal attitudes toward Native American communities. The act aimed to relocate Native American tribes living east of the Mississippi River to lands west of the river, primarily to open more land for white settlement and cultivation, particularly with the booming cotton industry driving demand for land.

This policy echoed a prevalent ideology of Manifest Destiny, which justified expansion across North America as inevitable and divinely sanctioned. Despite the economic motivations, the moral ambiguity of forcible relocation laid bare a national conflict.

The ramifications of the Indian Removal Act were severe and far-reaching. The policy led to the displacement of thousands of Native Americans, epitomized by the arduous and deadly

Trail of Tears journey that resulted in the suffering and loss of thousands of lives.

Tribes such as the Cherokee, Creek, and Seminole faced the dismantling of their societies, the erosion of their cultures, and the obliteration of their autonomy. This act highlighted the stark moral dilemmas faced by a nation grappling with its expansionist desires juxtaposed against principles of justice and human dignity (McNamara, 2020).

Opposition and Legal Resistance

Public sentiment against the Indian Removal Act was not uniform, however. There was notable opposition that marked early societal activism for indigenous rights. Figures such as John Ross, the Cherokee Nation's principal chief, resisted through legal channels, resulting in focal court cases such as *Worcester v. Georgia*.

These cases highlighted the tension between state and federal authorities, where the Supreme Court sided with Native American sovereignty, though Jackson infamously disregarded judicial rulings, reflecting the complex interplay of power between branches of government (The Editors of Encyclopaedia Britannica, 2025a).

While the act furthered the concept of American exceptionalism in practice, it also spotlighted glaring inconsistencies between American democratic ideals and the realities of marginalization and disenfranchisement faced by non-white communities. This period marked a significant point when national identity began intertwining with policies in such a way that projected both hope and hypocrisy.

Legacy and Transition to Lincoln's Leadership

The legacy of the Monroe Doctrine and the Indian Removal Act significantly shaped national identity and foreign policy. The Monroe Doctrine established America's role as a mediator in Western Hemisphere affairs, evolving into the 20th-century view of the region as America's backyard. In contrast, the Indian Removal Act exposed the contradictions in American ideals, compelling future generations to balance expansion with equity.

Next, we'll look into President Abraham Lincoln's leadership during the Civil War, discussing unity and division during crises. The early policies of his predecessors set the stage for the war's causes and informed Lincoln's governance, illustrating his enormous influence on historical leadership and contemporary policy-making.

Lincoln and the Preservation of the Union

In the previous section, we explored the complex dynamic of American identity through the Monroe Doctrine and the Indian Removal Act. These events laid the groundwork for an era rife with complexity and a nation on the precipice of transformation.

The Civil War era, defined largely by Abraham Lincoln's presidency, magnifies these issues of unity and division. Lincoln faced perhaps the most daunting task of preserving a nation fractured by regional loyalties and ideologies. His leadership during this national crisis serves as a quintessential study of unity against significant divisive forces.

Lincoln's Vision of Unity

Lincoln entered his presidency in a time when the very essence of American identity was uncertain. The Confederate states, determined to safeguard their social and economic traditions, challenged the principles of unity and democracy. Under threat of secession, Lincoln's vision remained steadfast: He sought to preserve the Union at all costs.

His speeches demonstrated an extraordinary ability to articulate the concept of a singular, unified nation. In his first inaugural address, Lincoln implored his countrymen to remember their shared history, urging them to act with the understanding that they were not enemies but friends (Swanson, 2022).

Balancing Firmness and Empathy

Balancing firmness with empathy, Lincoln's leadership expressed the emotional gravity of American identity. His second inaugural address, only months before his assassination, exemplified this balance.

He articulated a vision that went beyond mere victory or defeat, appealing to the higher ideals of healing and rebuilding a nation with these words: "With malice toward none, with charity for all, with firmness in the right as God gives us to see the right" (*Lincoln's Second Inaugural Address*, 2022). This approach underlined his understanding of the Civil War as not just a military struggle but also a strong moral crucible that would determine the nation's future (Hahn & Morlando, 1979).

Redefining the War's Purpose

Lincoln's strategic decisions during the Civil War were seminal in redefining the war's purpose. The Emancipation Proclamation emerged as a landmark decision, signaling a shift in the Union's style and message. It reframed the war as a battle for freedom and equality, rather than merely a quest to preserve the Union.

This transformed the war into a moral struggle and altered its political and social landscape. By redefining the objectives, Lincoln secured the moral high ground and helped to disintegrate the Confederacy's socio-economic foundation built on slavery.

His strategic acumen extended beyond this proclamation. He maneuvered a turbulent political environment, making choices that influenced both military tactics and political legitimacy. His adeptness at assembling a capable military leadership, as seen in the appointment of Ulysses S. Grant, catalyzed a series of decisive victories that would ultimately lead to Union triumph. However, this complicated coordination of military strategies and political obligations was fraught with trials (History.com Editors, 2025a).

Opposition and Division

The opposition Lincoln faced very much highlights the division challenging unity. Conflicts in his cabinet, vacillating public opinion, and intense political pressure tested Lincoln's resolve. The Peace Democrats, or Copperheads, as they were called at the time, vociferously opposed the war, sharply criticizing Lincoln's policies and further exacerbating national discord.

Division in his cabinet lingered, as many advisers harbored conflicting visions for the nation's future. Yet, through patience, dialogue, and steadfastness, Lincoln managed these internal disputes.

The pressures were not confined to his immediate political sphere. Across the nation, ideological and emotional rifts persisted. There were factions in the Union that questioned Lincoln's decisions, and his re-election campaign was marked by intense scrutiny and doubt. Despite these challenges, Lincoln's re-election in 1864 demonstrated his superior leadership and the people's faith in his vision of unification (Searles, 2024).

Legacy of Unity and Reconstruction

Lincoln's presidency inarguably left a lasting imprint on American identity. His commitment to unity and principled stand during the Civil War set the stage for the reconstruction and reconciliation processes that followed his assassination.

His strategic brilliance and moral clarity during this national crisis helped to build a new narrative for America, one where ideals of freedom and equality were more than abstract concepts but guiding principles for the nation's evolution.

Even today, Lincoln's legacy invites cultural discourse and reflection. His presidency was a turning point in the American narrative, setting a precedent for presidential authority and leadership in times of national threat. The unresolved issues of unity and division during his era resonate with contemporary politics, offering lessons on governance amid adversity.

Examining Lincoln's strategies reveals how the Civil War era shaped American society's trajectory. His leadership echoed the United States' ongoing journey toward reconciling foundational ideals with divisive realities, a process that, while fraught, steadily progressed toward unity.

Andrew Johnson's Struggles During Reconstruction

As we move to later periods of American history, the themes of unity and division persist. President Andrew Johnson's challenges during Reconstruction were deeply rooted in the societal rifts highlighted by Lincoln. Unlike Lincoln, Johnson faced intensified divisions in the post–Civil War era, as his efforts to unify the nation confronted ongoing resistance.

After the death of Abraham Lincoln, the mantle of leadership fell to Andrew Johnson, thrusting him into a period of intense national change known as Reconstruction. Unlike Lincoln, who had been a master of political compromise and had worked tirelessly to hold the Union together, Johnson entered this role with contrasting instincts and vision.

His presidency illuminated consequential aspects of national identity and sectional divides that emerged prominently during Reconstruction.

Johnson's Approach to Reconstruction

Initially seen as a symbol of Southern Unionism, Johnson's campaign for the White House coincided with rising expectations. Uniting the country required piloting the extremely tense and complex landscape of post–Civil War America. Yet, where Lincoln sought collaboration, Johnson's tenure was marked by discord with Congress and a different ideological approach to Reconstruction (Varon, 2016).

He believed emancipation merely meant freedom without extending broader citizenship rights, a view that reflected his staunch belief in the supremacy of white citizenry and maintained the prewar social order—except for the institution of slavery (Varon, 2023). This perspective created a significant rift, with Congress pushing for expanded rights and protections for the newly freed African Americans.

Legislative Battles and Power Struggles

The legislative battles between Johnson and Congress highlighted a key shift in power dynamics, increasingly driving the nation into further division. Johnson's presidency became notorious for its vehement clashes over Reconstruction legislation, such as the Freedmen's Bureau Bill and the Civil Rights Act of 1866. His use of veto power against these measures illustrated a deep constitutional struggle.

For instance, Johnson's veto of the Civil Rights Act was emblematic of his resistance to policies promoting racial equality, contributing to legislative conflicts that Congress responded to with overwhelming veto overrides. This era marked a moment when the legislative branch asserted itself, counteracting what it saw as executive overreach and underscoring the deepening division over civil rights (History.com Editors, 2025b).

Leniency Toward the South and Black Codes

Johnson's vision for the post-war South involved leniency toward former Confederate states, allowing them significant autonomy in their reconstruction processes. This leniency extended to policies that permitted states to enact Black Codes, laws designed to restrict the freedom of African Americans and secure their availability as a cheap labor force.

As a result, Johnson hindered progress toward race equality and entrenched systemic discriminatory practices that continue into the present day. The societal impact of his Reconstruction policies was especially pronounced for African Americans who faced curtailed civil rights and socioeconomic opportunities (The Editors of Encyclopaedia Britannica, 2024a).

Resistance to Black Empowerment Movements

The reignited empowerment movements that advocated for Black suffrage and civil rights met considerable resistance during Johnson's presidency. His ideological stance and policies were perceived as an endorsement of the status quo pre-war racial hierarchy. As a consequence, these movements faced significant obstacles and hostility, resulting from an official unwillingness to embrace and enforce extensive reforms for racial equality.

The chaos of Reconstruction under Johnson provided fodder for those already skeptical of racial equality as a national policy, influencing public opinion and policy decisions well beyond his term (*Historicizing Black Resistance in the U.S.*, 2024).

Historians' Perspectives of Johnson

Historians have interpreted Johnson's legacy with a wide variety of results, frequently viewing it with criticism but recognizing its complexity. Labelled politically inept, Johnson demonstrated an inflexibility that made him a polarizing figure. Nevertheless, his presidency serves as a reminder of the challenges and opportunities inherent in the governing landscape of post-war America.

While Johnson may have lacked Lincoln's finesse in negotiation and adaptation to a changing political climate, his presidency reflects the fledgling nation's ongoing struggle with equality and justice (Varon, 2023).

Lessons From Johnson's Presidency

In evaluating Johnson's presidency against the broader scope of U.S. history, his failure to reconcile competing national interests and his inability to adequately address the deep-rooted racial issues shed light on the persistent quest for civil rights and unity.

Johnson's contentious legacy shows the potential perils of leadership lacking vision and dynamism in times of critical transition. Reflecting on this period offers critical lessons on how entrenched societal divides can hamper progress and emphasizes the leadership responsibilities in achieving national cohesion.

The relationship between Johnson's policies and his clashes with Congress significantly shaped the national discourse on identity and equality. His presidency shows how political and racial dynamics, when mishandled, can define national identity for generations.

Amid the backdrop of studying Reconstruction, we can observe the beginning of many modern debates surrounding civil rights and federal authority, issues that remain at the forefront of American politics. Understanding Johnson's era in the context of Reconstruction serves as a framework to deal with similar contemporary challenges.

Concluding Thoughts

The legacies of Presidents James Monroe, Andrew Jackson, Abraham Lincoln, and Andrew Johnson illustrate the complexities of American identity and foreign policy. Monroe's Doctrine established the US as a dominant force in the Western Hemisphere, while Jackson's Indian Removal Act highlighted the moral dilemmas in America's expansion. Lincoln's presidency during the Civil War was marked by his vision of unity and compassion, striving to preserve the nation amid division.

Conversely, Johnson's Reconstruction era faced challenges from resistance to civil rights, revealing the ongoing struggles between ideals of equality and historical injustices. Together, their actions molded the nation's trajectory toward reconciliation and identity.

In the next chapter, we'll look at how Teddy Roosevelt's trust-busting initiatives reshaped the presidency's role in economic affairs, highlighting the tensions of Taft's challenges and Wilson's transformative reforms.

Chapter 2 National Unity and Division

Chapter 3

Presidential Responses to Industrial Growth and Social Change

The Progressive Era saw the United States grappling with extensive changes sparked by industrial growth and social upheavals. This chapter explores how Presidents Theodore Roosevelt, William Howard Taft, and Woodrow Wilson faced these challenges head-on. By scrutinizing their antitrust policies and economic reforms, we uncover their attempts to balance corporate power with public welfare, offering insights into leadership during an era striving for fairness amid complexity.

Chapter 3 Presidential Responses to Industrial Growth and Social Change

President Theodore Roosevelt: A Leader of Change

After serving in the New York State Assembly, Theodore Roosevelt became the Assistant Secretary of the Navy and later gained national attention through his leadership of the Rough Riders during the Spanish–American War in 1898. His military success catapulted him into the national spotlight, ultimately paving the way for his election as the 26th President of the United States in 1901 (*Theodore Roosevelt*, 2024).

Presidency and Progressive Reforms

Assuming the presidency after the assassination of William McKinley, Roosevelt brought with him a fervent belief in progressivism, emphasizing the need for social reform and the advancement of the common man. He championed various social causes, including labor rights, women's suffrage, and consumer protection.

Roosevelt was known for his energetic approach to leadership, famously stating that he aimed to "speak softly and carry a big stick." This method shaped his foreign policy, leading to significant accomplishments like the construction of the Panama Canal and the negotiation of peace in the Russo-Japanese War, for which he won the Nobel Peace Prize in 1906 (Gould & Mooney, 2023).

Trust-Busting Efforts

One of President Roosevelt's most significant legacies is his commitment to curbing corporate greed through trust-busting.

In the early 1900s, many American industries were dominated by large monopolies, which stifled competition and exploited consumers. Roosevelt believed that while big businesses were vital for the economy, they should not be allowed to wield excessive power that harmed the public interest.

He took a measured approach, selectively targeting trusts rather than waging a war against all corporations. The Northern Securities Company, a powerful railroad trust, became one of the first major targets of his administration. Under the Sherman Antitrust Act, Roosevelt successfully dismantled the company, demonstrating his willingness to stand against corporate giants (*The Trust Buster*, n.d.).

His administration pursued several other notable cases against trusts, including the beef and oil industries, earning him the reputation of a trust-buster. However, his efforts were not without criticism. Some viewed him as overreaching in his enforcement of antitrust laws, while others believed he was being too lenient. Nevertheless, Roosevelt's legacy in this area laid the groundwork for future regulatory reforms, highlighting his role as a president who sought to balance the interests of business with the welfare of the nation.

Taft's Approach to Trust-Busting

Taft's presidency marked a significant continuation of the antitrust policies initiated by Theodore Roosevelt. By expanding trust-busting efforts, Taft made it clear that he believed in using the law to challenge corporate greed and enforce regulatory frameworks.

Chapter 3 Presidential Responses to Industrial Growth and Social Change

Taft's Inclusive Approach to Antitrust

Unlike Roosevelt, who selectively targeted trusts, Taft's style was more inclusive. He initiated more antitrust lawsuits than Roosevelt, emphasizing a strict legal stance against monopolistic practices. This increase in prosecution reflected changing expectations about presidential authority in the economic sphere.

Taft clearly communicated that the government intended to play a more active role in market regulation, stressing law enforcement's importance in curbing market manipulation and protecting consumers (Ginsburg, 2021).

The Payne-Aldrich Tariff

Taft's presidency wasn't without its controversies, notably the Payne-Aldrich Tariff. Taft signed this tariff into law in an effort to lower rates, but the resultant bill fell short of expectations. The tariff turned out to be more protective than reformative, infuriating progressives who saw it as a betrayal of their ideals (McClung, n.d.).

Originally a progressive effort to lower tariffs and encourage fair competition, this legislative undertaking deviated significantly from its reformist goals. Influential figures such as Senator Nelson Aldrich and Representative Sereno E. Payne managed to push through a tariff bill with only modest reductions, ultimately undermining Taft's intentions and alienating reformist supporters. This reversal exposed fractures in Taft's political alliances and ignited discontent among progressive Republicans (Arnold, 2025).

This controversy emphasizes the limitations of Taft's reforms, revealing underlying tensions in the progressive movement. It highlighted the inherent complexities in political alliances necessary for enacting reform and illustrated the challenges Taft faced in remaining true to progressive ideals while managing political realities.

Public Perception and Challenges

Taft's popularity often suffered compared with Roosevelt's, whose charismatic personality and bold policies had set a high bar. In contrast, Taft appeared more conservative and cautious, characteristics that the public didn't respond as positively to. Public perception played a critical role in reform initiatives, as reflected by Taft's struggle to maintain the same enthusiastic support for his measures as his predecessor had (Korzi, 2021).

His presidency became a cautionary tale about the obstacles reform-minded leaders often face, including fragmentation in their parties. Taft's struggles to bridge divides in the Republican Party exemplified the broader challenges of leading while trying to manage an evolving political landscape and its expectations.

Contributions to Antitrust Enforcement

Despite numerous challenges, Taft made central contributions that fortified antitrust enforcement frameworks. He established a legal precedent on which future administrations could build, developing a more thorough regulatory mechanism aimed at tackling monopolistic enterprises.

By rigorously pursuing corporations through the judiciary, Taft reinforced the idea that the government bore the responsibility to counteract corporate dominance. While his tactics contrasted in execution from Roosevelt's approach, the overarching commitment to reform made clear the administration's dedication to regulating big business for the greater public good (Bittlingmayer, 2011).

Chapter 3 Presidential Responses to Industrial Growth and Social Change

Contradictions in Leadership

Taft's presidency might be characterized by contradictions, but it also reflected the intricacies of leadership during a period of reform. His tenure illustrated the multifaceted nature of public expectations amid political changes.

On the one hand, he advanced antitrust laws; on the other, he struggled to handle the political alliances necessary to further the wide array of progressive reforms that various factions had demanded. Unlike his dynamic predecessor, Taft often appeared as a leader mired in complexity, attempting to balance hefty reforms while remaining cautious (Korzi, 2003).

The Dual Legacy of Taft's Presidency

The dual legacy left by Taft includes both his enforcement of antitrust laws and the political challenges he grappled with. His administration set foundational regulatory practices that outlasted his presidency, yet it also highlighted the importance of political strategy and public relations in achieving political objectives. The lessons from Taft's tenure serve as a reminder of the nuanced nature of leadership during transformative periods in American history.

Building upon Roosevelt's legacy, Taft felt that antitrust reforms were obligatory while dealing with the era's industrial growth. He stood poised to address the complexities inherited from his predecessor, including the burgeoning corporate monopolies. Roosevelt's dynamic policies had placed a spotlight on corporate regulation, marking a watershed in the executive branch's responsibilities.

Inheriting this context, Taft faced the job of maintaining the momentum while confronting deeper societal and economic shifts.

Intensified Antitrust Efforts

Taft's administration notably intensified the frequency and scope of antitrust lawsuits. Roosevelt had solidified his reputation as a formidable trust-buster by initiating groundbreaking legal actions. However, in an effort to advance these efforts, Taft pursued a more extensive litigation program, filing more antitrust lawsuits than Roosevelt had. These actions underscored Taft's commitment to impose law on monopolistic enterprises and challenge corporate practices threatening market competition (Woerner, 2023).

Cases such as the prosecution of Standard Oil and the American Tobacco Company exemplify Taft's aggressive stance. These legal battles, initiated during Roosevelt's tenure but vigorously pursued under Taft, demonstrated an emphasis on dismantling large corporations that manipulated market conditions. His administration's lawsuit against the American Sugar Refining Company further illustrated his determination in combating corporate monopolies regardless of their powerful influence (Admin, 2025).

Political Struggles and Internal Discord

Politically, Taft grappled with the delicate balance required to sustain his reformist momentum. His efforts to implement progressive legislation often got entangled in political disputes that eroded public perception of his presidency.

The dismissal of Gifford Pinchot, a devout conservationist closely linked with Roosevelt, marked another contentious episode. This decision emphasized the internal discord in his administration and highlighted his struggles in corresponding fully with progressive ideologies (Bushong, 2012).

Chapter 3 Presidential Responses to Industrial Growth and Social Change

Taft's inability to maneuver the political minefield effectively reduced his appeal across the political spectrum. Many Progressives viewed his administration's concessions as betrayals, leading to diminished support in his own party. His perceived failure to fully realize the progressive ideals initiated by Roosevelt left Taft grappling with declining approval, despite his advances in antitrust litigation.

The Legacy of Antitrust Enforcement

Nevertheless, Taft's presidency set about defining groundwork for future administrations' antitrust enforcement. His pursuit of a legal framework thorough enough to challenge and dismantle monopolistic corporations left behind a legacy for the economic reforms that followed. While contemporary public opinion often overshadowed his contributions, his administration's focus on solidifying legal precedents in corporate regulation endured as a focal aspect of his legacy.

Examining Taft's presidency reveals a period rife with administrative dualities and public expectations. His tenure encapsulates the inherent tension between maintaining reform aspirations and directing the complexities of political realities.

While his presidency faced substantial hurdles, his legacy of legal integrity in trust-busting shaped the trajectory of presidential economic interventions well beyond his administration.

Next, we'll examine how Taft's presidency transitions to Woodrow Wilson's administration. While Taft emphasized legal rigor, Wilson introduced Progressive Era reforms focused on economic and social change. His policies redefined presidential roles, aiming for significant shifts in economic regulation and societal reforms.

Wilson's tenure marked a new chapter for the Progressive Era, addressing systemic issues through extensive policy measures. The next section will explore how Wilson's ideals built upon the foundations laid by Roosevelt and Taft.

Wilson and the Progressive Era Reforms

Taft's presidency marked a notable period for antitrust enforcement, and this foundation paved the way for Wilson's New Freedom Program. Taft vigorously pursued legal action against monopolistic corporations, filing more antitrust lawsuits than his predecessor, Theodore Roosevelt.

His administration's decisive trust-busting efforts aimed to break up conglomerates and restore competitive markets, which fed the American public's desire for fair economic practices. This groundwork of enhancing regulatory frameworks set the stage for Wilson's more ambitious reform agenda. He entered office with a vision to further dismantle corporate control and encourage economic equality.

Wilson's New Freedom Program

Wilson's New Freedom Program targeted the large industrial and financial corporations' monopolistic stranglehold on the economy. Unlike his predecessors, Wilson championed a philosophy of small government and decentralized power. His policies aimed to create a fairer economic environment by encouraging competition and limiting the influence of big businesses.

Mandatory to his agenda was breaking up monopolies to provide smaller businesses an opportunity to thrive. Wilson's style was less about curbing corporate power through government intervention and more about reinstating market conditions conducive to genuine competition, reconciling with his vision of a more democratic economic system (The Editors of Encyclopaedia Britannica, 2007).

Federal Trade Commission

A necessary aspect of Wilson's strategy was the establishment of the Federal Trade Commission (FTC) in 1913. The creation of the FTC represented a systematic shift toward regulated commerce and the monitoring of business practices. The commission was designed to prevent unfair methods of competition and to protect consumers from deceptive practices.

By instituting a government body with the authority to investigate and take action against unethical business practices, Wilson significantly altered corporate governance and how it functioned. The FTC became a key element in safeguarding the public and ensuring that companies adhered to rules that furthered fairness in the marketplace (Kazin, 2020).

The Clayton Antitrust Act

Simultaneously, Wilson reinforced antitrust legislation through the Clayton Antitrust Act of 1914. This act built upon prior laws by providing further protections against monopolistic practices. Unlike the Sherman Antitrust Act, which was often criticized for its ambiguity, the Clayton Act introduced specific prohibitions on corporate behaviors that stifled competition, such as price discrimination and exclusive dealings.

It also protected labor unions by exempting them from being categorized as monopolies, which was groundbreaking in accommodating labor rights with antitrust law. This increased focus on legislative detail reinforced Wilson's commitment to addressing the complexities of antitrust enforcement and reducing the concentration of corporate power (Beaubouef, 2023).

Economic and Social Reforms

Wilson's economic reforms were intimately tied to social progress. His administration pushed for labor rights, successfully enacting laws that were meant to improve the working conditions of American laborers. One such achievement was the Adamson Act, which established an eight-hour workday for interstate railroad workers. This was a significant step in labor reforms and demonstrated Wilson's dedication to the rights and well-being of workers during a time when industrialization often meant exploitation.

On top of that, his support for the eventual successful passage of the Nineteenth Amendment, advocating women's suffrage, highlighted his administration's impact on social equality (Rust, 2025b). This commitment to societal issues illustrated how deeply economic reforms were intertwined with broader social progress during this era.

Impact and Challenges

Wilson's policies present both significant achievements and notable challenges. The regulatory frameworks he implemented led to tangible changes, such as increased prosecution of unfair business practices and greater empowerment of consumers in the marketplace. However, these measures faced resistance from corporate giants and certain political factions, who argued that such regulations stifled business innovation.

Despite this, Wilson's reforms encouraged a shift in legal precedents that expanded the role of government in economic matters and led to advances such as improved labor standards and more inclusive voting rights (Ambar, 2023).

The Federal Reserve Act

As we transition toward discussing the Federal Reserve Act, it is important to note its critical role in Wilson's overall strategy, providing the United States with a safer and more flexible monetary system. Unlike previous attempts at monetary reform, this act established a centralized banking system designed to offer financial stability and distribute monetary power more evenly.

By creating a system that adjusted the supply of money and managed interest rates, the Federal Reserve Act helped establish economic stability and steadiness, both of which had been previously lacking. This move toward centralized banking oversight was necessary in laying the groundwork for future economic securities and will be elaborated upon next.

The Legacy of Wilson's New Freedom Program

Wilson's New Freedom Program marked a transformative era in American economic policy by championing competitive markets and introducing legislation aimed at reining in corporate power while addressing social inequalities. Although the implementation of these policies faced challenges, Wilson's administration laid a critical foundation for future reforms.

His efforts emphasized the possibility of harmonizing economic and social progress, creating a legacy of reform that subsequent administrations would build upon. The narrative continues with the exploration of the Federal Reserve Act, shedding light on how it introduced a new era of centralized monetary policy to guarantee economic resilience and stability.

The Federal Reserve Act's Impact

Continuing from Wilson's New Freedom Program and the establishment of the Federal Trade Commission, we see the Federal Reserve Act emerge as an indispensable instrument of economic governance in the Progressive Era. The Act, enacted in 1913, addressed the urgent need for a decentralized yet coordinated monetary system, heralding a new era of economic reform and oversight.

During this period, there was a broad recognition among reformers of the instability plaguing the American banking system, particularly the recurrent bank panics that had far-reaching economic repercussions. The Federal Reserve System was established to inject stability into this volatile landscape.

A Flexible and Sturdy Banking Framework

What made the Federal Reserve Act so critical was its approach to building a flexible yet robust banking framework. Decisively, it established the Federal Reserve as America's central bank, tasked with controlling the money supply, thereby providing the government with a more sophisticated monetary policy toolset.

The creation of Federal Reserve notes introduced a much-needed elasticity to the currency, vital for the economic calamities of the time. This new form of currency, incorporated with the existing money supply, helped to create a more predictable and controlled response to fluctuations in economic activity (Wheelock, 2021).

Instilling Public Confidence

The intent of this legislation extended beyond mere stability; it sought to instill public confidence in the nation's financial system. The centralization of banking oversight minimized the likelihood of systemic failures, thereby catering to the broader public's needs and concerns about their financial security.

The Federal Reserve's role in discount window lending affirmed its status as a lender of last resort, ensuring liquidity when it was critically needed. This function proved indispensable, particularly during periods of crisis when other financial institutions were unable or unwilling to provide credit.

Economic Cooperation and Planning

Beyond these foundational aspects, the Federal Reserve Act established unprecedented economic cooperation and planning. By adjusting discount rates and manipulating the purchase and sale of government securities, the Federal Reserve began influencing macroeconomic conditions in an effort to balance economic growth with financial stability.

This proactive stance on monetary policy, though relatively rudimentary at the time, laid the groundwork for the sophisticated economic management practices of the future (Chen, 2024).

The Great Depression and Subsequent Reforms

One of the Act's significant implications was its impact during the Great Depression. Despite some criticism for failing to mitigate the severity of the Depression, the Federal Reserve's existence and framework provided a foundation upon which later reforms could build. The legislative changes during and after the Depression, such as the Banking Act of 1933, can be seen as extensions and modifications of the original Act's intent.

These reforms further solidified the Federal Reserve's role in economic stability and restored public faith in financial institutions by, for example, introducing the Federal Deposit Insurance Corporation (FDIC) to safeguard deposits (Richardson, 2013).

World War II and the Treasury Accord

Through successive administrations, the presence of the Federal Reserve became a cornerstone in U.S. economic policymaking. World War II provided another litmus test; the Fed's actions in support of war financing demonstrated its capability to adapt and manage economic goals in tandem with national priorities.

The Treasury Accord of 1951, which came after the Korean War, highlighted tension and eventual reconciliation between the goals of the Treasury and the Federal Reserve, emphasizing the latter's independence and much-needed role in shaping monetary policy. This independence remains an important aspect of its modern functioning, allowing it to act independently of daily political pressures (Sanches, 2013).

Chapter 3 Presidential Responses to Industrial Growth and Social Change

Contemporary Relevance

The Federal Reserve's adaptability, as evidenced over the decades, illustrate its importance in responding to economic crises. Indeed, the concept of central banking has evolved significantly, yet the underpinning principles of the Federal Reserve Act remain pertinent. This evolution finds contemporary relevance in how the Federal Reserve dealt with the financial challenges of the 21st century, specifically during the 2007–2008 financial crisis and, later, the COVID-19 pandemic.

Adaptive measures such as adjusting interest rates, unconventional monetary policies, and broadening lending facilities reiterated its commitment to fulfilling its dual mandate of promoting employment and stabilizing prices (Wheelock, 2021).

Each phase of the Fed's history reaffirms its indispensable role in preserving economic order. While initially born from a necessity to quell banking panics and stabilize note issuance, its responsibilities now encompass a wide range of economic standards and practices that affect both national and global economies.

The mechanisms it pioneered—or adapted—such as managing the money supply and setting interest rates, have become embedded in U.S. economic policy. This institutional legacy signals not just historical continuity but also an ongoing responsibility to innovate and respond to emerging financial challenges.

The Progressive Era's Foundations

The Progressive Era's embrace of government intervention, epitomized by the Federal Reserve Act, marked a historic shift toward a more hands-on approach to managing the economy. As economic challenges evolve, so, too, does the Federal Reserve, reflecting the vision of economic equilibrium and public welfare envisioned by its creators.

This adaptability ensures it remains a foundation of economic policy, continually shaping and being shaped by the various socioeconomic forces at play across different administrations and eras.

Concluding Thoughts

This chapter examined the approaches of Presidents Theodore Roosevelt, William Howard Taft, and Woodrow Wilson during the Progressive Era, focusing on their antitrust policies and economic reforms. Roosevelt's selective trust-busting laid the groundwork for regulation, while Taft's legal actions advanced the fight against monopolies, despite political challenges.

Wilson built on these efforts by advocating for competitive markets and fairness, establishing the Federal Trade Commission and the Clayton Antitrust Act. Understanding their responses to economic challenges reveals how past leadership shaped government roles in regulation, influencing today's debates on corporate power and regulatory oversight in balancing innovation and societal welfare.

In the next chapter, we will explore FDR's New Deal and its influence on economic recovery, examine Truman's contentious decision to use atomic weapons, and analyze the societal shifts brought by Eisenhower's interstate highway system.

Chapter 3 Presidential Responses to Industrial Growth and Social Change

Chapter 4

Depression, War, and Recovery

In the 1930s, as the Great Depression cast its shadow over America, despair became a reality for many. Families faced unemployment and financial ruin, with breadlines and soup kitchens commonplace. Parents watched helplessly as their children went to bed hungry, and communities struggled to maintain hope amid economic hardship.

Factories fell silent, fields lay fallow, and stores shuttered, portraying a nation in distress. Amid these struggles, President Franklin D. Roosevelt's New Deal emerged, aimed at stabilizing the economy. By addressing immediate relief and long-term reform, it redefined the government's role and provided a framework for tackling future economic crises.

Chapter 4 Depression, War, and Recovery

FDR's New Deal and Infrastructure Reforms

As the United States weathered the Great Depression, Franklin D. Roosevelt's New Deal emerged as a symbol of hope for economic reform. This revolutionary initiative, introduced between 1933 and 1939, sought to rescue the faltering economy, offering immediate relief while setting the groundwork for long-term recovery.

Roosevelt's policies provided a template for future government interventions during economic downturns, illustrating a shift from laissez-faire governance to a regulated economy aimed at stability and balance.

The First 100 Days

The New Deal unfolded during the first 100 days of Roosevelt's presidency, a period characterized by swift legislative action. The crisis demanded immediate solutions, and Roosevelt's administration responded with programs targeting various sectors. One of the most significant reforms was the creation of the Works Progress Administration (WPA), which employed millions of jobless Americans.

This initiative stimulated economic activity by funding infrastructure projects, including 650,000 miles of roads and public buildings. The Civilian Conservation Corps (CCC) offered another avenue for employment, engaging thousands of young men in reforestation and flood control, thereby both providing work and preserving the environment (The Editors of Encyclopedia Britannica, 2025c).

The Social Security Act and Addressing Financial Instability

The Social Security Act of 1935 established the blueprint for the contemporary welfare system in the United States. By establishing a national old-age pension system, the Act provided financial security to the elderly and unemployed, reducing the vulnerability of these groups to economic fluctuations. This program signaled a required shift in federal responsibility, as it cemented the government's role in individual welfare, ensuring that citizens would not be left entirely to the whims of economic cycles (Wall, 2016).

In addition to direct relief efforts, the New Deal addressed systemic financial instability. For instance, the Banking Act of 1933 included the establishment of the Federal Deposit Insurance Corporation (FDIC), which insured depositors' accounts. By guaranteeing the safety of bank deposits, the FDIC helped restore public confidence in the financial system, encouraging savings and investment (Heakal, 2024).

The Securities Act of 1933 introduced government oversight in stock trading, aiming to prevent the speculative excesses that contributed to the market crash of 1929. These reforms were integral to stabilizing the financial sector and reducing the likelihood of future crises (Kenton, 2024).

Agricultural Reforms

The agricultural sector also received significant attention under the New Deal. The Agricultural Adjustment Act (AAA) sought to stabilize prices by paying farmers to reduce production. This effort, while controversial, attempted to curtail surpluses and raise farm product prices, offering relief to a demographic severely impacted by the Depression (*Agricultural Adjustment Act*, 2024).

The Tennessee Valley Authority (TVA) exemplified another facet of agricultural reform, bringing cheap electricity and modern infrastructure to rural areas, which improved agricultural productivity and living standards (Wilmoth Lerner, 2025).

Uneven Distribution of Benefits

Despite these achievements, the distribution of New Deal benefits was uneven. While these programs alleviated some economic distress, they frequently discriminated against racial minorities and women, who did not reap the same level of benefits as white men. Yet, it is important to recognize that women achieved symbolic breakthroughs during this era, and African Americans attained more advantages from Roosevelt's policies than from any administration since Abraham Lincoln's.

Through the correspondence of these disparate groups with the Democratic Party, the New Deal coalition emerged as a force in American politics, underpinning the Democratic agenda for decades (Braik, 2018).

Legacy of the New Deal

Although the New Deal did not single-handedly end the Great Depression—World War II would ultimately spur complete recovery—it established a foundation that made American capitalism less volatile. By extending federal regulation into new areas such as labor and industry, it laid a precedent for contemporary economic recovery practices. Programs such as the Social Security Act continue to influence today's policies, underlining the longevity and impact of Roosevelt's reforms (Rust, 2025a).

The New Deal's legacy lies in the concrete programs it initiated and in its transformation of the nation's politics. By advocating for a government-regulated economy, it offered a balanced approach between free enterprise capitalism and complete state control.

This ideology became a core principle of modern American economics, furthering an environment where government intervention could mediate market failures and protect the welfare of its citizens.

Next, we'll uncover how the development of infrastructure initiated by Franklin D. Roosevelt's New Deal and expanded under Eisenhower's interstates drove socio-political and economic evolution. As the country moved forward, these highways emerged as vital conduits for growth and progress.

A Highway System and Economic Transformation

The legacy of Franklin D. Roosevelt's New Deal initiatives laid a foundation for transforming American infrastructure, which eventually led to the expansive interstate highway system developed under Eisenhower. The New Deal's attention to infrastructure stimulated a climate of government-led development, embracing a vision where infrastructural growth could drive sociopolitical and economic evolution throughout the nation.

This vision undoubtedly influenced Eisenhower, who saw the development of highways as a means of connecting cities and states, important for national security and socioeconomic progress during the Cold War era.

Suburbanization and Cultural Shifts

Eisenhower's interstate highway system served as a catalyst for upgrading transportation across the United States, directly influencing major social dynamics. It created pathways for suburbanization, reshaping where Americans lived and how they commuted. By linking rural areas to urban centers, the highways spurred the growth of suburbs, encouraging migration away from congested city centers to more expansive suburban homes.

This migration pattern also created cultural shifts, as families found new ways to interact socially and economically, adapting lifestyles to accommodate suburban living. The ease of travel opened up opportunities for new businesses and industries along highway routes, further integrating commerce into everyday life (Eschner, 2017).

Economic Value and Job Creation

On the economic front, the highways advanced substantial economic value by improving the efficiency of freight transport, reducing costs and time, which directly stimulated commerce. The ability to efficiently move goods across the country was vital. Businesses could access wider markets, and regions previously isolated by poor infrastructure could now engage in broader economic activities.

The construction of the highway system itself created millions of jobs, proving that large-scale government projects could drive economic prosperity during uncertain times. The reach of these highways encouraged investment in areas once deemed too remote for development, triggering a cascade of economic opportunities (Capka, 2006).

Strategic Military Importance

Amid these economic transformations, the strategic military importance of the highways during the Cold War cannot be overstated. In the geopolitical climate of the time, there was an acute awareness of the need for rapid military mobilization. Eisenhower, a military man himself, recognized that an extensive highway network would allow for quick movement of military personnel and equipment, thereby enhancing national security.

These highways were designed to accommodate military vehicles and tanks, ensuring that troops could be deployed quickly across the nation in the event of an emergency. This dual-purpose strategy, where civilian infrastructure also served military needs, represented an innovative intersection between national development and defense strategy (*Eisenhower's Highways*, 2024).

Revitalizing Cities and Logistics Innovations

In exploring specific impacts, we can see how the highway system revitalized cities that were previously considered outposts by connecting them to larger metropolitan areas. The economic revitalization of these cities is directly tied to their newfound accessibility, which encouraged tourism and business development.

The interstate system also paved the way for logistical innovations. Shipping companies began to rely more heavily on trucks for freight, leading to the exponential growth of industries surrounding logistics and warehouse management (History.com Editors, 2025d).

Social Implications

The implementation of the interstate highway system also connected to broader social implications. For many Americans, this network signified more than just roads—they now had access to new opportunities and the promise of a better life. As commuting became easier, people could consider jobs and educational opportunities farther afield, thereby indirectly contributing to an increase in educational attainment and career advancement opportunities.

This newfound connectivity was not without its challenges, particularly in addressing socioeconomic disparities, but it laid a critical infrastructure on which America could build (*Exploring the History of the Interstate System*, 2024).

Cold War Preparedness and Multifunctional Infrastructure

As America's involvement in the Cold War deepened, the strategic edge these highways could provide helped to cement the notion that the US was strong and prepared. Being able to swiftly respond to threats was not just reassuring to the public but also critical to maintaining a strong defense posture against the Soviet Union.

The complete integration of strategic utility into a project meant for civilian use showed a time when infrastructure was viewed as having multiple functions, highlighting how investments in public works could offer dual-use benefits (Black, 2018).

Transition to the New Frontier

The development of interstate highways during the Kennedy administration set the stage for civil rights movements and economic restructuring, including future efforts focused on improving society and promoting equality. The New Frontier was poised to leverage the infrastructure advances made previously, aiming to build greater social inclusion and economic opportunity.

Infrastructure developments like President Dwight D. Eisenhower's highways illustrated the successful interaction between mobility and progress, ushering in subsequent waves of policy reform focused on bridging inequality and expanding economic horizons.

Roads as Conduits for Change

The change brought on by roads and highways illustrates the interconnection between physical infrastructure and the evolving sociopolitical landscape, setting the stage for initiatives under Kennedy aimed at breaking down barriers and opening up pathways to equitable growth. As America progressed toward the 1960s, the achievements of past administrations demonstrated an understanding that integrating infrastructure with social change could drive significant transformations.

Infrastructure and Social Changes

Understanding the broader narrative of overcoming crises leads us to explore consequential leadership decisions and their far-reaching impacts, particularly as the changes in infrastructure and society during the 1960s reshaped governance and civic engagement. President Harry Truman's decision to utilize atomic weapons significantly altered global diplomacy, establishing the United States as a formidable power but also inciting tension and an arms race.

The use of atomic weapons against Japan in 1945 aimed to hasten the end of World War II. Faced with the prospect of immense casualties from a ground invasion, Truman authorized the bombings of Hiroshima and Nagasaki, believing it would save lives and ensure a swift victory.

President John F. Kennedy's New Frontier initiatives emerged against this backdrop, aiming to tackle domestic challenges and shift societal norms. The New Frontier emphasized space race dynamics alongside educational investments, reflecting a strategic vision to rejuvenate American progress through innovation and equality.

The Space Race and Technological Advancements

Kennedy ignited the race to space, propelled the nation's technological capabilities, indirectly driving economic growth and job creation. The creation of NASA and the drive to land a man on the moon were emblematic of overcoming technological and ideological barriers during a time of Cold War anxiety.

This focus on technology made its way into civilian sectors, leading to advancements that would shape the digital revolution and today's tech-driven economy. By pushing boundaries in space exploration, Kennedy also reinforced the broader ethos of striving for equality and progress, fueling civil rights activism (Ostovar, 2024).

Educational Investments and Societal Growth

Educational investments, a driving force behind the New Frontier, aimed to build a skilled workforce and bridge societal divides. The Higher Education Act of 1965, although posthumously aligned with Kennedy's vision, channeled funds into universities, making higher education accessible to underrepresented groups.

This shift laid foundational blocks for societal change, fueling civil rights movements by empowering marginalized communities with knowledge and resources. By investing in education, Kennedy advanced the notion that societal growth is linked to inclusive empowerment, echoing today's emphasis on educational equity (Palmadessa, 2023).

The Civil Rights Movement and Legislative Action

The Civil Rights Movement during Kennedy's era was greatly boosted by his support, albeit cautious, serving as a major engine for societal transformation. His administration's endorsement of the Civil Rights Act of 1964 signaled critical federal backing for racial equality. This landmark legislative action outlawed discrimination, breaking barriers and creating societal ripple effects felt to this day.

The synergy between Kennedy's New Frontier and civil rights efforts underscored his administration's understanding that breaking racial barriers was integral to America's promise of prosperity and equality (*The Modern Civil Rights Movement*, 2022).

Economic Opportunity and Global Leadership

Kennedy's focus on economic opportunity intersected with his technological and educational investments. Initiatives such as the Peace Corps and Alliance for Progress depicted a vision of using American resources for global betterment, promoting socioeconomic development in underprivileged regions (*Alliance for Progress*, 2021; *Peace Corps*, 2024).

These efforts spotlighted the interconnectedness of American global leadership and domestic prosperity, arguing that uplifting others in the global community translates to mutual growth. American leadership, as framed by Kennedy, involved both portraying opportunities abroad and ensuring economic equity at home.

Legacy of Innovation and Equality

In many ways, these movements and initiatives created pathways for future development, connecting past challenges to contemporary successes. The digital era, driven by technological advances, roots itself in the spirit of innovation captured during Kennedy's time. The persistent quest for equality parallels the civil rights advances sparked in the 1960s, while educational equity remains a critical agenda, responding to Kennedy's vision of uplifting through knowledge.

Patterns of Leadership and Societal Impact

A closer look at these themes reveals the delicate interaction between leadership, societal progress, and global standing. Kennedy's New Frontier arguably laid the groundwork for modern America, advocating for education, challenging technological frontiers, and confronting social injustice.

His legacy illustrated that presidential actions wield the potential to mold social structures, proving that genuine progress often arises from visions of equity and inclusion. By analyzing these historical movements, we discern patterns of leadership that inspire contemporary efforts to overcome crises and achieve equitable progress (The Editors of Encyclopaedia Britannica, 2020a).

The Power of Investment

The implementation of Kennedy's initiatives demonstrated the power of investment in human capital and technology. By prioritizing these sectors, his administration built strength against economic downturns, echoing today's emphasis on continuous innovation and education as mechanisms for sustainable growth. The reinforced belief is that handling economic and societal challenges requires proactivity in advancing opportunity and embracing progression.

The confluence of Kennedy's initiatives reshaped how international relations and domestic policies were envisioned. As globalization became inevitable, strengthening innovation and nurturing human potential turned into critical strategies to maintain economic competitiveness. Kennedy's administration foresaw these changes, setting the stage for an America defined by its technological achievements and commitment to diversity and inclusion (Hald-Mortensen, 2007).

Visionary Leadership and Long-Term Impacts

Kennedy's New Frontier initiatives demonstrate the relationship between leadership choices and long-term societal effects. Kennedy envisioned an America where technological advancement, educational access, and equal opportunity were not just democratic ideals but also tangible goals. His presidency epitomized a critical period during which deliberate action against crises laid the groundwork for future paths, standardized with broader themes of recovery and progress.

This exploration of Kennedy's efforts suggests that overcoming crises calls for visionary leadership that links immediate actions with long-term societal impacts. His New Frontier initiatives remain relevant, highlighting the importance of combining innovation with equity to contribute to a society poised to tackle forthcoming challenges.

The story of recovery and advancement echoes through these policy decisions, tracing a narrative where leadership decisively shapes societies for generations. Through understanding and analyzing Kennedy's era, one comprehends the need for strategic vision in overcoming adversity, fueling hope for an equitable future.

Concluding Thoughts

The New Deal's socioeconomic reforms redefined government roles during hardships and helped us understand presidential decisions like Truman's atomic strategy and Kennedy's New Frontier. Roosevelt's governance shifts established a framework for managing domestic challenges and engaging in global conflicts. Past innovations in economic stability and infrastructure paved the way for today's crisis management and peace-building.

Lessons from domestic governance and global diplomacy shape strategies for equitable and lasting policymaking. Educators and students can draw parallels to current crises, contemplating how past lessons can inspire future leadership and social progress.

In the next chapter, we'll explore how LBJ's Civil Rights Act reshaped American society by establishing legal equality while examining Nixon's complex stance on desegregation and Ford's commitment to affirmative action.

Chapter 4 Depression, War, and Recovery

Chapter 5

Civil Rights Leadership

Picture a young teacher in her small classroom in the Deep South during the 1960s. She prepares for another day of teaching as civil rights marches echo outside, demanding equality. Inside the school walls, outdated textbooks and policies resist these changes. Today's lesson reminds her of the hope sparked by the Civil Rights Act of 1964, which promised to reshape classrooms by prohibiting discrimination.

The teacher understands that real change is slow. The era's tension between progress and persistence illustrates the importance of presidential leadership in advancing civil rights, setting the stage for further reforms in America.

In the next section, we'll see how President Lyndon B. Johnson's Civil Rights Act and the Great Society programs collectively transformed American society. We'll examine the ambitious goals of these initiatives aimed at addressing systemic poverty and racial injustice, the criticisms they faced, and their undeniable impact on the civil rights movement.

Investigating the complexities of Johnson's legacy, we'll also consider how his efforts reshaped discussions around equality and justice in the United States, setting the stage for subsequent generations of activists.

LBJ's Civil Rights Act and Great Society

Lyndon B. Johnson's presidency marked a significant epoch in American civil rights history, principally due to the passage of the Civil Rights Act of 1964. This piece of legislation outlawed discrimination based on race, color, religion, sex, or national origin, thereby setting rigorous legal standards for equality in the US. Johnson, with his political acumen, skillfully overcame congressional resistance, drawing on both moral arguments and sincere determination to push the Act through.

His efforts galvanized a nationwide push for civil rights, emboldening activists and setting high expectations for future legislation and social reform (Gittinger & Fisher, 2023).

The Great Society Program

At the heart of Johnson's vision for America was the Great Society program, an ambitious set of domestic policies designed to address poverty and racial injustice. His initiatives spanned various domains but notably centered on education and healthcare—two areas mandatory in resolving socioeconomic disparities, which were long intertwined with racial inequalities.

The Higher Education Act of 1965, for instance, expanded access to higher education through financial assistance, aimed at leveling the educational playing field for marginalized communities. Medicare and Medicaid, introduced in 1965, extended healthcare coverage to the elderly and the impoverished, significantly helping economically disadvantaged minorities and reducing healthcare-related inequalities (Freidel & Sidey, 2015).

By focusing on socioeconomic reform alongside civil rights, Johnson strived to dismantle the underpinnings of racial injustice. His approach provided immediate relief to many disadvantaged Americans and laid the groundwork for a societal shift toward greater equity. By tackling these systemic issues head-on, Johnson's Great Society programs prompted subsequent legislative efforts aimed at closing racial and economic gaps.

Criticism and Impact

Johnson's civil rights agenda wasn't without its critics. Some argued that the breadth and speed of his reforms resembled a "shotgun approach," where poorly thought-out policies were rushed through Congress. Despite these criticisms, Johnson's reforms were undeniably a product of the tightrope of political compromise and necessity. His policies dramatically improved the quality of life for countless Americans, exemplified by the sharp decline in poverty rates from 19% in 1960 to 12% by 1969 (Iceland, 2015).

Specific measures of public well-being, such as infant mortality rates and access to healthcare, showed marked improvements during Johnson's administration. These outcomes highlight the substantial societal impact of his policies, despite criticisms regarding their execution.

Chapter 5 Civil Rights Leadership

A Complicated Legacy

The legacy of Johnson's leadership in civil rights is complicated. On the one hand, he made substantial strides in integrating American society, from appointing African Americans to key positions of power to passing groundbreaking civil rights and voting legislation. These actions symbolized a broader commitment to encouraging a more inclusive nation, both legally and culturally.

On the other hand, his presidency saw significant domestic unrest, particularly in urban areas where systemic inequalities remained deeply entrenched, and this change was resisted heavily. While the legislative framework for equality was strengthened under Johnson, the persistent challenges of implementation and enforcement highlighted the limits of political reform alone in addressing deep-rooted social issues (Bennet, n.d.).

Reshaping the Civil Rights Dialogue

Johnson's initiatives contributed significantly to reshaping the effects and definition of civil rights in America, through legislation and changing the dialogue around racial equality and justice. His presidency established a renewed governmental commitment to civil rights, inspiring future generations to continue pushing for progress. Yet, the social tensions of the era, coupled with the Vietnam War's shadow, complicated Johnson's legacy, balancing substantial achievements with an era of national turmoil.

Next, we'll examine how Nixon and Ford dealt with the complexity of civil rights policies, focusing on Nixon's controversial busing initiatives and Ford's commitment to affirmative action. Both presidents shaped the trajectory of desegregation efforts in a divided nation, setting the stage for future advancements under Jimmy Carter's administration.

Nixon's and Ford's Policies

As we now look at President Richard Nixon's approach to desegregation and busing and Ford's policies, we'll examine how Johnson's momentum affected these policies. Inheriting a divided nation on civil rights, Nixon faced challenges in advancing desegregation, particularly in education. His presidency focused on controversial busing initiatives, addressing the lasting issues of inequality and discrimination built upon Johnson's foundation.

Nixon's Busing Policy

Nixon's foray into civil rights, particularly school desegregation, demonstrated a mix of strategy and hesitation. His administration confronted the challenge of integration in education, a task that remained thorny despite the Civil Rights Act of 1964 and the prior Supreme Court decision in Brown v. Board of Education.

While taking steps toward a more unitary school system, Nixon's efforts were tempered by his cautious stance on busing, a method that hugely impacted desegregating schools (*Nixon's Record on Civil Rights*, 2022). His approach, though well-intentioned, met significant resistance locally and among various public sectors, further highlighting the complexities in enforcing civil rights reforms at the federal level.

Chapter 5 Civil Rights Leadership

Ford's Civil Rights Policies

When President Gerald Ford assumed office, he inherited a changing political environment regarding civil rights. Ford's presidency is notably marked by a commitment to affirmative action, continuing Nixon's somewhat reluctant push toward equality in new directions.

Ford's administration saw affirmative action not merely as a policy initiative but also as a moral obligation to boost diversity across sectors. This era expanded the concept of civil rights beyond mere desegregation, focusing on creating tangible opportunities for marginalized groups (Gonyea, 2013).

Affirmative Action and Representation

Ford endorsed initiatives aimed at increasing the representation of African Americans and other minorities in various territories, from education to the workplace. This commitment translated into policies that unequivocally supported affirmative action, acknowledging that equality required active participation rather than mere proclamations of intent.

His tenure also witnessed an effort to diversify the federal government, with Ford recognizing that representation begins at the top. The political climate, partly shaped by Nixon's tenure, needed to be handled with great caution, where promoting rights meant more than enacting laws; it involved actively dismantling systemic barriers.

The Nixon Pardon

However, Ford's presidency was not without controversy or difficulty. His decision to pardon Nixon remained divisive, casting a shadow on his administration's ethical policies. Critics argued this act compromised justice and suggested leniency toward political indiscretions, potentially undermining civil rights successes by eroding trust in federal leadership.

Nevertheless, Ford maintained a focus on human rights—the foundation of civil rights—and strove to clarify his position that this pardon was intended to help the nation heal and move forward (Coyne, 2024).

Shifting Republican Attitudes Toward Equality

In terms of civil rights, Ford's legacy underscores an important change in Republican attitudes toward equality, illustrating the party's fluctuations between tradition and progressive reforms. His vision of human rights extended internationally, articulating American moral standards on a global stage. This global focus laid groundwork that influenced Americans, as well, establishing a link between international human rights advocacy and domestic civil rights achievements.

A Commitment to Human Rights

This transition connects perfectly into the Carter administration, which pushed the boundaries of civil rights into broader definitions involving international human rights activities. Ford's influence on this shift was undoubtedly tremendous. His policies, while having faced criticism, left a mark that encouraged a continued strong federal response to equality and justice issues—a dual focus that Carter would continue to develop (History.com Editors, 2025f).

Ford's Role in Shaping Civil Rights

Ultimately, Ford's presidency played a compelling role in shaping the role of civil rights in the late 20th century. His policies and leadership style helped redefine federal responsibility in ensuring civil rights, emphasizing active participation in rectifying disparities and promoting diversity. While his decisions, particularly the pardon of Nixon, were contentious, Ford's strong commitment to affirmative action and human rights contributed a vital chapter to America's ongoing quest for equality.

Moving forward, it becomes evident that Ford's initiatives laid the ground for Carter's strengthened dedication to human and civil rights. This continuity ensured the civil rights momentum did not falter, despite the political and social tumult surrounding the Nixon era's conclusion. Carter's administration capitalized on these foundations, demonstrating that while leadership styles may differ, the end goal of equality remains a constant pursuit.

Bridging Civil Rights Efforts

As we transition to Jimmy Carter's era, it bears noting how deeply the legacies of the preceding administrations shaped his policy choices. Carter's more explicit emphasis on human rights, both nationally and internationally, built on Ford's work and carried it into new arenas.

Ford's emphasis on human rights and diversity prepared a backdrop for his successor, President Jimmy Carter, who took office with a strong commitment to these ideals. The evolution of civil rights during the Ford administration informed Carter's subsequent actions. Ford's efforts set the stage, yet Carter's administration amplified the commitment to human rights, creating policies and laws that became more embedded in American policy both at home and abroad.

Gerald Ford's presidency was pivotal in American civil rights during a time of unrest and shifting societal expectations. His administration brought a new tone to Republican discourse on civil rights, influencing future policymakers. Ford's support for affirmative action and human rights showed his commitment to racial equality and the belief that true prosperity must include marginalized communities.

He emphasized the importance of human rights in both domestic and international contexts, with his involvement in the 1975 Helsinki Accords promoting collaboration among nations and empowering activists in Eastern Europe. Ford's controversial pardon of Nixon reflected his focus on national healing, prioritizing collective well-being over political interests (Richmond, 2014).

His administration advanced gender equality by appointing women to key positions and fighting against discrimination. Ford's legacy influenced future administrations, particularly Jimmy Carter's emphasis on human rights, marking a significant shift in political discourse toward a more inclusive approach to civil rights.

Carter's Human Rights Advocacy

Drawing connections between Carter's commitment to human rights and its impact on the Civil Rights Movement builds an understanding of how leadership can influence societal change. Carter's tenure, which leapt off from Ford's human rights efforts and kept running with it, marked a period rife with change, both internationally and domestically. His agreement with the Helsinki Accords, which emphasized human rights, framed his foreign policy and reinforced civil rights principles at home.

Intertwining Foreign and Domestic Policy

During this era, the intertwining of foreign and domestic policy became increasingly evident. Carter's presidency came at a time when the global struggle for human rights was gaining momentum. The Jackson–Vanik amendment, part of 1970s U.S. foreign policy, exemplified how American legislative efforts targeted human rights beyond its shores.

This amendment restricted financial and trade incentives for countries that imposed emigration constraints, highlighting the US's stance against oppressive regimes and corresponding with Carter's agenda to champion human rights globally (Tyszkiewicz, 2022).

Strategic Use of Human Rights

Carter's national security adviser, Zbigniew Brzezinski, understood the strategic value of human rights as a tool to challenge Soviet ideologies. His efforts to leverage the Helsinki Accords opened up new platforms for the US to insist on these rights, forming a backdrop against which Carter's domestic civil rights policies were shaped.

The administration's focus on these accords demonstrated that foreign policy could deeply affect US policy. Carter's actions affirmed the principle that rights are universal and must be defended consistently, regardless of geography (Donnelly, 2024).

Expanding Civil Rights at Home

In the US, Carter's leadership coincided with ongoing struggles for equality. The late 1970s presented civil rights challenges that extended beyond race to include gender, disability rights, and more. By listening, learning, and understanding human rights, Carter paved the way for more inclusive policies.

His administration took deliberate steps to improve minority representation in governmental roles, thereby creating increased attention to multiple voices in government. This commitment to inclusivity made certain that the civil rights dialogue expanded to encompass broader social justice issues (Nittle, 2021).

Grassroots Movements and Global Advocacy

Carter's dedication to human rights also inspired grassroots movements. By integrating civil rights into broader human rights rhetoric, he provided a new language for activists to employ. This transnational perspective empowered nonstate actors across the globe, illustrating a domino effect in which advocacy in one sphere could incentivize similar actions elsewhere.

Indeed, the Helsinki network became a vital part of this movement, with its norms catching the attention of Western NGOs and influencing U.S. governmental policy to their advantage (Tyszkiewicz, 2022).

Public Awareness and Modern Governance

The impact of Carter's policies extended beyond mere legislation. His commitment increased public awareness regarding the importance of government accountability in civil rights enforcement. Modern governance continues to reflect his influence, with policies focusing on equity being urgent to contemporary dialogues.

The precedence set during his presidency emphasizes the continuity of human rights as a part of civil rights advancements, guiding current policy-making processes toward more inclusive practices. Analyzing the advancements during Carter's presidency demonstrates how effective leadership can influence both elite and grassroots levels.

As citizens gained greater empowerment through legislative reforms, they contributed to shaping the increasing role civil rights played in the nation. Such changes underline the significance of top-down commitment to rights that then fuel bottom-up activism, encouraging persistent dialogue and action around equality.

A Blueprint for Fairness and Justice

Carter's focus on human rights, as part of civil rights, presented a blueprint for how leadership can encourage an environment that is conducive to ongoing discussions about fairness and justice. His administration's policies did not merely react to injustices but actively sought to prevent them—a major shift in governance approach.

Through this leadership, Carter made sure that civil rights were continually addressed in contemporary dialogues, maintaining their relevance across generations. Presidential actions exert a deep-rooted effect on civil rights. As seen through Carter's initiatives, leadership decisions reverberate through time, shaping sociopolitics.

His human rights–centered style continues to inform current debates around equality, proving that such leadership can extend its impact far beyond its tenure. The emphasis on international human rights reinforced the overarching themes of civil rights, illustrating the interconnectedness of policies aimed at stimulating equity on a global scale.

A Legacy of Inclusive Governance

Carter's human rights emphasis, in domestic and international domains, set a crucial precedent for integrating these rights into the broader civil rights framework. His presidency exemplifies how strategic alliances and legislation can nurture an inclusive approach to governance.

It's clear that a commitment to inclusive human rights can serve as a vital foundation for civil rights leadership, advancing dialogues and developments well into the future. Through Carter's pioneering policies, the integration of these issues has left a great legacy, invigorating modern efforts for justice and equality (Tyszkiewicz, 2022).

Concluding Thoughts

Lyndon B. Johnson, Richard Nixon, Gerald Ford, and Jimmy Carter collectively shaped the civil rights environment in America, each contributing distinct perspectives and policies. Johnson's Civil Rights Act and Great Society initiatives established a framework for equality, while Nixon understood and worked through the complexities of desegregation and busing. Ford continued this momentum with a strong commitment to affirmative action and human rights, despite controversies surrounding his Nixon pardon.

Chapter 5 Civil Rights Leadership

Carter further expanded the civil rights dialogue by intertwining human rights within domestic and foreign policy, advocating for broader inclusivity. Together, these presidents built a legacy that emphasized the ongoing pursuit of social justice and equality.

In the next chapter, readers will explore Reagan's intricate defense strategies, George H.W. Bush's pivotal Gulf War leadership, Clinton's engagement in NATO expansion, and the many implications of the Berlin Wall's fall.

Chapter 6

Cold War Challenges

In this chapter, we examine U.S. presidential strategies during the Cold War, focusing on how these approaches shaped international relations and military policies. Ronald Reagan's presidency marked a significant shift with the Strategic Defense Initiative, a technological leap aimed at countering Soviet threats. This bold initiative ignited a strong public discourse, revealing a nation divided between innovation and fiscal responsibility used during the Cold War, focusing on how these approaches shaped international relations and military policies. Ronald Reagan's presidency marked a significant shift with the Strategic Defense Initiative, a technological leap aimed at countering Soviet threats. This bold plan ignited a strong public discourse, revealing a nation divided between innovation and fiscal responsibility.

As we progress through various presidents' administrations, including George H. W. Bush and Bill Clinton, we explore how their diplomatic engagements, military interventions, and economic strategies responded to the changing geopolitical structure, ultimately bridging historical precedents with contemporary challenges.

Cold War Strategies and Military Initiatives

President Ronald Reagan's leadership was marked by a dramatic shift in U.S. strategy during the Cold War, particularly through the introduction of the Strategic Defense Initiative (SDI). Announced in 1983, SDI sought to develop a sophisticated missile defense system intended to shield the United States from potential Soviet nuclear attacks.

This initiative represented a bold leap into advanced technology domains, typifying a distinct shift from traditional deterrence strategies to one prioritizing technological superiority. The SDI, often dubbed "Star Wars," reflected America's commitment to maintaining a technological edge in global military capabilities.

Public and Political Discourse

The proposed defense system spurred significant public and political discourse. Critics questioned its feasibility and cost, arguing that the project might turn into a financial sinkhole without guaranteeing definitive protection. Opponents in and outside the United States feared it could spark a new arms race, exacerbating already tense US–Soviet relations (The Editors of Encyclopaedia Britannica, 2025e).

Meanwhile, supporters hailed it as a necessary step into the future, advocating for the importance of innovation in national defense tactics. Reagan's initiative symbolized the broader ideological clash of the era: the struggle between heavily investing in technological advancements and addressing concerns over ballooning military expenditures.

Financial Prioritization and Economic Impact

From a financial perspective, Reagan's administration prioritized military spending, significantly increasing the budget for defense projects, including the SDI. This surge was part of a broader strategy to assert military dominance, countering the Soviet threat with overwhelming might and capability. By investing heavily in the military-industrial complex, the administration aimed to fortify national security and stimulate economic growth by creating defense-related jobs.

This infusion of funds into the defense sector had rippling economic effects, leading to increased employment opportunities, particularly in technology and defense industries. The spending policies, while aimed at cementing U.S. superiority, also evoked debates around fiscal responsibility. Critics pointed to potential neglect of domestic issues due to an imbalanced focus on military readiness (Dobson, 2005).

Diplomatic Engagement and Arms Reduction

Diplomatically, Reagan's era marked a central change in US–Soviet relations. Despite his hawkish defense policies, Reagan engaged in several high-profile negotiations with Soviet leaders that eventually laid the groundwork for arms-reduction treaties. Notably, his meetings with Mikhail Gorbachev, the current, and, ultimately, last leader of the USSR, demonstrated the administration's dual strategy of combining intensive defense preparedness with deliberate diplomatic efforts.

The Reykjavik Summit of 1986, though initially ending without agreement due to disputes over the SDI, ultimately paved the way for the 1987 Intermediate-Range Nuclear Forces (INF) Treaty and later arms-reduction agreements (Hunt, 2017). These negotiations emphasized that strong defense positioning could coexist with diplomatic engagement, underscoring the administration's strategy to balance a strong military with arms-control dialogue.

The Cultural Impact of the Arms Race

The arms race significantly impacted American culture and public perception, heightening societal fears and anxieties. The era saw an increase in civil defense drills and the proliferation of media content highlighting nuclear anxiety. Films and literature often depicted dystopian futures dominated by nuclear holocausts, mirroring public unease about potential military escalations.

Public awareness campaigns sought to familiarize civilians with survival strategies, though these often inadvertently increased paranoia, showcasing how deeply military strategy permeated everyday life. All forms of culture during this time reflected a nation grappling with the implications of living under the perpetual threat of nuclear conflict (Kimball, 2004).

Legacy and Influence on Geopolitical Dynamics

Reagan's strategies and the outcomes of his initiatives would greatly influence geopolitical dynamics, especially in how subsequent administrations approached Cold War tensions. Although heavily criticized, the SDI exemplified the notion of using technological advancements as strategic assets, a concept echoed in later defense strategies.

As Reagan's term ended, his military posture and diplomatic engagements established a foundation that President George

H.W. Bush would inherit, especially as Bush piloted complex international situations, such as the Gulf War. The era's legacy illustrated the significance of integrating innovative technology with traditional military and diplomatic tactics, ensuring strategic flexibility in confronting evolving geopolitical challenges (Fischer, 2010).

Reshaping Cold War Politics

Reagan's presidency fundamentally reshaped the nature of Cold War politics by emphasizing a blend of technological innovation, increased defense spending, and diplomatic engagement. These strategies illustrated the complexities of Cold War tensions and laid the groundwork for future policymaking when dealing in international relations and military strategy.

As the narrative moved toward Bush's leadership and its impact on US–Soviet relations, Reagan's strategies remained relevant, demonstrating the tremendous influence of his policies in shaping historical and contemporary geopolitical dynamics.

Transformation in Geopolitical Alliances

Reflecting on George H. W. Bush's leadership during the Gulf War brings into sharp focus the evolution of American military strategy and international relations as the 20th century came to a close. Bush's Gulf War leadership was instrumental in reshaping U.S. strategies, marking a transition point that President Bill Clinton's administration further built upon in the post–Cold War era.

Chapter 6 Cold War Challenges

The US involvement in the Gulf War showed off an international coalition-building approach and a shift toward multilateral military engagements, establishing a precedent that subsequent administrations respected, setting the stage for Clinton's strategic policies.

NATO Enlargement and Collective Security

As the geopolitical landscape transformed with the Cold War's end, Clinton's foreign policy was characterized by adapting to this new global context. The strategic rationale behind NATO's enlargement was central to his diplomatic agenda.

By admitting former Eastern Bloc countries into NATO, the Clinton administration aimed to guarantee stability and deterrence in Eastern Europe, a commitment to collective security that sought to manage the region's volatility through a strategic lens. This decision was part of a broader strategy to secure peace and develop democracy in Eastern Europe (Knott, 2025).

The expansion addressed security concerns relating to Russia's influence and was necessary in reassuring newly democratic nations of their place in the West. This agreement provided the US with strong strategic allies, reinforced America's commitment to defending its interests and those of its allies, and highlighted a significant shift toward preventive diplomacy to mitigate potential conflicts.

Diplomacy and Democratic Engagement

Clinton's policies emphasized diplomacy and collaboration over confrontation, and these were reflected in initiatives that boosted democratic values and built partnerships with emerging democracies. These strategies marked a departure from the hardline stances of previous decades, illustrating a cautious approach to international relations. For example, Clinton's administration actively engaged in diplomatic efforts across Eastern Europe, promoting economic and democratic reforms.

This engagement sought to nurture stability and discourage the resurgence of authoritarianism while aiming to unite these nations into the global economy and community, thereby reinforcing democratic governance as a pillar of American foreign policy (Søndergaard, 2015).

NATO Expansion as a Strategic Tool

The North Atlantic Treaty Organization (NATO) expansion initiative, in particular, served as both a symbolic and practical reinforcement of diplomatic and military strategy. NATO membership offered Eastern European countries a security guarantee that was critical to their development as sovereign, democratic states.

Expanding NATO also allowed the US to project power and influence diplomatically without direct confrontation, coinciding with Clinton's broader foreign policy strategy. This approach reflected a strategic shift from reactive to preventative measures, focusing on creating a security framework that discouraged aggression through a united defensive posture (Lapsley & Vandier, 2025).

Military Interventions in the Balkans

Transitioning to military interventions, Clinton's approach in the Balkans further signified a recalibrated U.S. role on the global stage amid the post–Cold War transition. The Bosnian conflict, characterized by humanitarian crises and ethnic cleansing, presented a dilemma balancing national sovereignty and humanitarian intervention.

Facing international pressure to act, Clinton's administration began military interventions in Bosnia and Kosovo. These actions highlighted the complexities of intervention in regional conflicts, especially in balancing humanitarian needs with broader geopolitical stability. U.S. leadership in NATO operations in this region underscored its role in enforcing peace through both diplomatic and military means (Daalder, 2024).

Controversies and Challenges

Clinton's interventions were not without controversy. Critics argued about the challenges of engaging in conflicts where national interests were not overtly threatened. These interventions were perceived as a test of validity for the emerging international order, where global consensus and multilateral action were the focal points. However, they also enforced the idea that post–Cold War foreign policy required adaptability to address non-traditional threats, such as ethnic conflicts and humanitarian crises.

In examining these interventions, it becomes evident that they were focal in redefining America's role in global conflict resolution. The Balkan engagements showed the world a willingness to intervene in complex situations, prioritizing international justice and humanitarian concerns in coalition with allies. While it did boost the concept of American leadership in global peacekeeping, these interventions also sparked debates over sovereignty, intervention rights, and the ethical dimensions of military involvement (Riley, 2023).

Globalization and Trade Policies

Clinton's policies provide a clear economic perspective on the evolution of U.S. foreign policy. Amid the political and military domains, Clinton's efforts to combine global economies illustrated an extension of foreign policy to economic strategies.

These initiatives reflected a broader U.S. commitment to strengthening global economic growth and stability—not just through political alliances, but also by promoting free trade and open markets. By focusing on globalization, Clinton aimed to position the US as a leader in the new global economy, emphasizing the interconnectedness of the world and the need for cooperative economic policies.

Legacy of Clinton's Foreign Policy

Clinton's foreign policy and NATO expansion are necessary in understanding the nuanced shifts in American strategy following the Cold War. These strategies were emblematic of a broader transition to addressing new global realities through diplomatic engagement, strategic alliances, and adapted military policies. They lay the groundwork for subsequent policies that continue to shape the international order.

End of the Cold War and Broader Implications

Clinton's foreign policy, particularly his advocacy for NATO expansion, set a stage that would ultimately frame the changing dynamics as the Cold War came to an end. Drawing from past

Chapter 6 Cold War Challenges

lessons, U.S. presidential strategies had to pivot sharply to reconcile with shifting geopolitical dynamics, creating new styles of engagement that sewed together remnants of the past while charting out future paths.

As various presidents became involved, their strategies reflected the complicated relationship between tradition and innovation, bending under the weight of historical experiences while grasping the future's potential.

Beyond the Iron Curtain

With Clinton, the emphasis on NATO enlargement represented an effort to expand democratic influence and stabilize Central and Eastern Europe. This strategy of inclusion worked to draw former adversaries into a collective security framework and projected American power and political ideals beyond the Iron Curtain.

Such moves were designed to mitigate potential power vacuums that could second-guess the US's economic and military dominance. By relaxing military tension and contributing to cooperation, Clinton's strategies influenced many international partnerships that became vital during the complex post–Cold War global environment.

Foundations in Cold War Strategies

Yet, the efforts Clinton laid out wouldn't have been feasible without anchoring earlier strategies that entrenched U.S. presence worldwide. Dwelling deeper into presidential strategies during the Cold War, it becomes apparent that each administration drafted policies interwoven with the intricacies of realpolitik and global competition. These decisions mirrored and strengthened key Cold War ideologies, ensuring multiple political fronts gestated under cautious stewardship (Sarotte, 2019).

Kennedy's Diplomatic Balancing Act

During the Kennedy administration, strategies revolved around the delicate balance of downscaling diplomatic tensions with the USSR while sidestepping the potential for direct military confrontation. This duality became especially apparent during the Cuban Missile Crisis, compelling both sides to negotiate a cautious détente without overt repudiation of their underlying antagonism.

Kennedy's maneuvers during this crisis highlighted the need for adeptness in negotiations, leaving a lasting blueprint that guided future leaders when engaging in high-tension encounters with other superpowers (Sherwin, 2020).

Nixon's Pragmatic Diplomacy

Meanwhile, Nixon's strategic reorientation displayed the life-and-death reshuffling of priorities. By embracing détente with the Soviet Union and encouraging bridging diplomacy with China, he opened unprecedented avenues for economic and political engagement. Nixon's approach reshaped the contours of Cold War diplomacy, illustrating the latitude given to transformative platforms that balanced rivalry with pragmatism.

His legacy proved the vast potential for reshaping international norms through carefully curated, albeit controversial, policy decisions that addressed global interdependencies (Shvangiradze, 2025).

Carter's Human Rights Emphasis

Carter's tenure reflected an era during which the weight of prior administrations' Cold War strategies was combined with human rights emphasized as a key tenet of foreign policy. His administration's armaments reduction efforts and push for international diplomacy, albeit with mixed results, emphasized the perennial balancing act between moral imperatives and strategic imperatives. Still, these efforts, whether wholly successful or not, helped highlight vulnerabilities in expansive military engagements (Cohen, 1982).

Reagan's Technological and Economic Strategy

Reagan's presidency came with its own unique cocktail of strategies that breathed life into Cold War confrontations, heightening an arms race that buttressed the ideological contrast between capitalism and communism. Through his well-publicized rhetoric and sweeping military programs, Reagan established a heightened awareness of American power.

His strategies pivoted toward economic and technological pre-eminence, as evidenced by actions such as the Strategic Defense Initiative, girdling political engagements with objectives that outpaced mere military considerations (Rowland & Jones, 2016).

Post–Cold War Realities

Looking back, the Cold War era demanded endless adaptability in strategy, each president adding new elements that catered to contemporary challenges while drawing from their predecessors' accomplishments and missteps. These transformations were neither linear nor predictable, as evident in the dissolution of the USSR, where efforts at containment eventually cascaded toward an entire region's liberation from a bipolar framework (Chivvis et al., 2024).

In this narrative, the transition between Cold War strategies and post–Cold War realities was marked by complicated diplomatic engagements, military involvements, and the recognition of global economic interdependencies. The Reagan–Gorbachev summits and ensuing arms-reduction treaties reflected an acknowledgment that sustainable global stability required concerted multinational cooperation.

Legacy of Cold War Strategies

By studying past strategic needs, modern foreign policy makers grasp for clues from their Cold War antecedents. The imprints of each strategic initiative during the Cold War created pathways that current U.S. presidents increasingly rely upon to maneuver an evolving geopolitical atmosphere.

Antecedent presidential strategies offer exemplars and warnings alike. Whether contemplating economic sanctions, building alliances, or projecting military might, today's geopolitical lenses remain etched with symbolisms borne out of the Cold War dialogues.

As the United States repositions itself in an increasingly multipolar world, the legacy of Cold War strategies continues to inform the narrative of presidential decision-making. These strategies illustrate a historical panorama of global diplomacy and conflict, framing the paradigms that guide modern American statecraft. From the Kennedy-era diplomatic crises to Clinton's expansions and beyond, these strategies serve as the foundation for current and future international policies.

Bridging Historical Precedents With Modern Challenges

Past presidential strategies, always complex and often adaptable, remain as relevant as ever. By bridging historical precedents with current exigencies, U.S. foreign policy can find pathways to not just survive but to act decisively amid global challenges and opportunities. Indeed, this direction, rooted in the learning gleaned from Cold War presidential strategies, encourages a coherent, albeit challenging, march toward a resignation with and renegotiation of American priorities on the world stage.

Concluding Thoughts

Having explored American presidential strategies during the Cold War, we can see how these historical maneuvers shape current global politics. Reagan established a post–Cold War world centered on innovation and alliance-building by emphasizing technological advances and combining military strength with diplomacy.

As educators and students study history, recognizing these patterns enhances our understanding of how past decisions influence contemporary governance and discussions. This awareness encourages critical examinations of leadership legacies while highlighting the importance of historical insights in modern international relations.

In the next chapter, we'll dive deeper into how presidencies have shaped political ideologies, focusing on the continuing impacts of the War on Terror, the Affordable Care Act, Trump's economic policies, and evolving environmental perspectives.

Chapter 7

Contemporary Ideological Shifts

In the aftermath of September 11, 2001, a wave of fear swept over the United States, altering people's sense of safety. Many people, once carefree New Yorkers, now anxiously checked the news daily, fearing another attack. Heightened security measures in their city provided mixed feelings; armed officers lined the streets, airports became fortresses, and conversations shifted from holiday plans to discussions about foreign threats.

This collective unease influenced national sentiments and policy decisions, making room for bold doctrines prioritizing national security. This chapter explores how these pivotal moments under recent presidencies reshaped political ideologies, paving the way for societal changes.

Chapter 7 Contemporary Ideological Shifts

George W. Bush's War on Terror

Examining the shifts stemming from President George W. Bush's War on Terror reveals its deep impact on American political thought, particularly regarding national security perceptions. This period created a more interventionist stance and reshaped policies, prioritizing counterterrorism over civil liberties. The aftermath of 9/11 sparked an intense sense of vulnerability, prompting the public to become more supportive of military actions abroad.

Politicians exploited this new outlook, leading to military interventions that were framed as necessary steps to secure American safety. Accordingly, the War on Terror became a battle against immediate threats and a struggle impacting political and public opinions about security and freedom (Sinnar, 2022).

Counterterrorism and Civil Liberties

The prioritization of counterterrorism led to significant shifts in public and political priorities, particularly around the delicate balance between security and civil liberties. Campaigns that emphasized national security garnered broader support as fear played a central role in influencing voting behaviors.

This societal shift influenced political discourse, as citizens spurred by fear and uncertainty gravitated toward leaders espousing stronger national security measures. In effect, fear became a potent political tool, standardizing public sentiment with interventionist policies that curtailed civil freedoms in favor of perceived safety (Hill, 2020).

Economic Anxiety

This period marked a rise in populist sentiments across the political spectrum, driven by disillusionment with established policies. Economic anxiety further exacerbated this discontent. The War on Terror's immense financial burden provoked discussions about governmental spending priorities, pushing citizens to question established political ideologies.

The convergence of economic and security concerns created fertile ground for populist leaders and movements, who leveraged dissatisfaction to challenge traditional party frameworks. For that reason, post-9/11 voter ideology increasingly reflected a desire to deviate from the status quo, furthered by anxiety over both fiscal and physical security (Bergmann, 2025).

Populism and Party Realignments

As it rose to prominence, populism challenged traditional party ideologies and expedited the formation of new political correspondence. As populist leaders highlighted economic concerns and disillusionment with existing political structures, they offered a narrative that the populace seeking change found highly relevant.

By tapping in to the unease surrounding economic uncertainties, these movements were able to unite disparate groups under a banner of reform. This led to shifts in party platforms as political entities adapted to the changing environment, often adopting more protectionist and isolationist stances.

Such realignments signaled an evolving political stage, reflecting broader shifts in voter priorities toward safeguarding domestic interests over international engagements (Curren, 2020).

Liberalism and Government Power

The War on Terror had a significant impact on liberalism, raising questions about the appropriate limits of government power in the name of security. The tension between civil rights and national security became a focal point of debate, with public sentiment heavily focused on surveillance, privacy, and due process. These issues permeated electoral outcomes, driving policy debates and partisan divisions.

Concerns about government overreach, heightened by policies such as the Patriot Act, fueled anxiety about the erosion of civil liberties. This dynamic challenged liberal ideologies, as questions of accountability and transparency came to the fore. Voters and policymakers found themselves grappling with the reconciliation of security needs with the protection of fundamental freedoms (Monten, 2005).

National Security vs. Democratic Principles

The tensions surrounding national security versus civil liberties manifested in a broader societal discourse, as efforts to protect the nation often collided with the values embedded in democratic principles. As a result, public debate became an arena for addressing these challenges, revealing the complexities of governance in an age of heightened threat perceptions.

This balance prompted vigorous discussions about the role of oversight and checks and balances, as well as the imperative of upholding constitutional rights. So, the War on Terror laid bare the relationship between government authority and individual freedoms in a rapidly changing world (Edicts Editorial Staff, 2024).

Bipartisanship and Polarization

Bipartisan support for initial military actions entrenched divides, creating a legacy of partisanship that continues to influence politics. This period saw a rare consensus in favor of security-oriented policies, with both major parties initially endorsing military interventions. However, as the costs and consequences of these actions became apparent, divisions emerged.

Public disillusionment with prolonged military engagements and the accompanying economic challenges sowed seeds of division within and between parties. As bipartisan enthusiasm waned, debates about the direction and ramifications of policies increasingly polarized the political climate, setting the stage for the contentious and fragmented discourse witnessed in subsequent years (Lee, 2024).

Policy Examples and Public Discourse

Concrete examples of these shifts can be seen in the implementation of policies such as the Department of Homeland Security's expansive surveillance measures, which sparked public discourse about privacy and governmental limits. Similarly, debates over the justification and consequences of military interventions in Iraq and Afghanistan symbolized broader battles about the role of the United States on the global stage and the true cost of the War on Terror.

These examples serve as reminders of the far-reaching consequences that security policies can have on a nation's political and philosophical framework, revealing the delicate nature of reconciling national interests with foundational democratic principles (Levinson-Waldman & Panduranga, 2021).

Chapter 7 Contemporary Ideological Shifts

Domestic Policy Priorities

As we transition to examining the shift toward health care reform, it is important to consider its implications for political discourse. This era's security-focused political realignments provide a backdrop for understanding subsequent shifts in public policy priorities, particularly as they pertain to domestic welfare and health initiatives.

The evolution from security-centric to health-centric debates marks a significant shift in politics, illustrating how emergent challenges continue to redefine priorities and reshape the terms of political engagement.

Obama's Affordable Care Act

The shifts following the War on Terror set the stage for complex political debates around health care reform, particularly with the introduction of the Affordable Care Act (ACA). The ACA aimed to expand health care access, fundamentally altering core political debates about health rights.

By promising to extend insurance to most uninsured Americans, the ACA reshaped discussions around governmental obligations and individual rights. It was a significant step toward viewing health care as a basic human right and was a critical point of contention in American political ideology.

This shift echoed through social institutions and relationships, strengthening the ties between citizens and the government but also complicating them.

Universal Health Coverage

Universal health coverage is the core principle of the ACA's promise. Although grassroots movements have historically focused on specific demands such as desegregating hospitals or releasing experimental medicines, there has long been a public undercurrent favoring broader health care reform.

The ACA, consequently, served as a focal point for both legislative and social movements, illustrating the divide between incremental changes achieved by prior grassroots efforts and a more comprehensive method of reimagining health care. This expansion brought about more intense social repercussions, as increased access to health care altered how people perceived their relationship to the state and one another (Harris, 2016).

The Government's Role in Health Care

The expansion of health care access through the ACA significantly affected perceptions of the government's role, leading to broader political discussions and debates. It brought questions about the extent of governmental involvement in citizens' lives.

Government intervention in health care was a practical solution for millions of uninsured people and became emblematic of a broader struggle. The lines were drawn more sharply between liberal values advocating for government intervention and conservative values upholding individual responsibility and free markets (Campbell & Shore-Sheppard, 2020).

Chapter 7 Contemporary Ideological Shifts

Partisan Tensions and Doctrinal Conflict

This divide further deepened partisan tensions. Over the years, the ACA evolved into a symbol of broader doctrinal conflict in America. While it signified progress for those who saw it as coinciding with fundamental liberties and rights, others viewed it as an overreach, sparking rigorous debates over health care policy.

The ACA became a legislative battleground for political differences, heavily influencing shifts in party platforms. Political alliances and oppositions started reflecting these changes, influencing party dynamics and electoral campaigns.

Grassroots Movements and Health Care Advocacy

Grassroots movements have played an increasingly significant role in these political dynamics. The civil rights movements, women's movements, and others have historically driven health care demands through specific agendas (Hoffman, 2011).

These movements responded to the ACA by either rallying around its advantages or critiquing perceived shortcomings, which in turn affected political platforms and strategies. For example, those advocating for universal coverage saw the ACA as both an achievement and a solid step toward more panoramic reforms.

Legacy and Social Welfare Precedents

The legacy of the ACA also set a precedent for future legislative emphases on social welfare, shifting public dialogue to recognize health care as an inherent right. Reform efforts like the ACA reveal a broader, evolving view of government in society—as both a protector and a provider. This gradual shift has opened doors for other social movements to leverage the ACA's standards in pushing for additional reforms in areas such as wage policies and racial equality.

Misinformation and Political Rhetoric

Amid all this, misinformation and political rhetoric began shaping public perception and opinion. The debate saw intense polarization, with confusion around the ACA being used as political ammunition on both sides.

Misinformation campaigns contributed to shifting public attitudes toward social safety nets and influenced voter mobilization strategies. Public opinion was significantly affected by the way political rhetoric framed these issues, leading to an electorate more divided but also more actively engaged in health care politics.

Electoral strategies adapted as parties recognized the sway health care held over voters. Campaigns began placing more emphasis on health care–related promises and reforms, viewing them as indispensable issues that could sway public opinion and, consequently, election outcomes. These strategies became central to political campaigns, with the ACA continually spotlighted in political discourse to rally support or opposition (Berinsky, 2015).

Broader Implications for Social Safety Nets

Looking forward, current debates around the ACA highlight its impact on public attitudes toward broader social safety nets. The continuous tug-of-war over its benefits and drawbacks within Congress and state governments showed the dynamic nature of health care reform and how it served as a catalyst for broader discussions on social policies. Understanding these discussions provides insight into their role as a pervasive thought running through recent political strategies.

Modern Conservatism

As a segue into evolving political ideologies, including Trump's economic policies' reshaping of modern conservatism, consider the ACA's ongoing role as a symbol of and vehicle for transformative social policy. It illustrates how intertwined health care debates are with other sociopolitical issues, forming a hotbed of discussion that influences economic and social policy formulations.

This tangled nature showcases how policy areas merge to influence broader narratives, shaping the future of American conservatism.

Trump's Economic Policies and Trade Wars

The Trump administration's economic policies marked a significant departure from the free-market principles traditionally associated with conservative economic thought. The "America First" agenda, central to Trump's economic strategy, emphasized protectionism and national interests.

This approach diverged from the more internationalist perspectives seen in prior administrations, such as President Barack Obama's, whose policies, such as the Affordable Care

Act, emphasized a more globalized outlook on economic and social issues.

Protectionism and Redefining Conservatism

Trump's approach to economic governance, particularly through the imposition of tariffs and renegotiation of trade agreements, redefined traditional conservatism by emphasizing protectionism over unrestricted free-market policies. By positioning tariffs as tools for negotiation and economic leverage rather than as fiscal policy instruments, Trump's administration reframed trade discussions within conservative circles.

This shift signaled a broader transformation, moving away from Reagan-era conservatism that had prioritized deregulation and minimal government intervention in economic affairs (Shongwe, 2025).

Impact on Rural and Working-Class Voters

The impact of Trump's economic policies on key demographics was extensive and complicated. For many rural and working-class voters, especially those who had felt neglected by previous administrations, Trump's focus on manufacturing growth and energy independence hit close to home.

Policies aimed at revitalizing the American manufacturing sector and reducing energy dependency were particularly appealing to rural constituents and labor forces affected by outsourcing and trade liberalization. By advocating for blue-collar jobs and prioritizing local industries, Trump tapped in to a reservoir of discontent among voters who felt left behind by globalization (Edsall, 2024).

Divides in the Republican Party

However, while these policies were hailed by segments of the white-collar working class, they also highlighted significant divides within the Republican Party. As economic nationalism took center stage, traditional conservatives raised concerns about abandoning free trade principles that had been long-standing tenets of Republican economic policy.

The tension within the party highlighted differing views on whether Trump's protectionism represented a necessary adaptation to modern economic challenges or a betrayal of core conservative values (Sun et al., 2025).

Legacy of Trade Wars

The legacy of Trump's trade wars presents a complex picture. Tariffs imposed on China and other trading partners aim to protect American industries but have led to mixed outcomes. While some sectors see short-term protection, American consumers may face higher prices on imported goods. Industries reliant on global supply chains experience disruptions and increased production costs, prompting debates on the efficacy of such protectionist measures (Wile & Murphy, 2025).

These developments intensify ongoing discussions on the role of globalization, with some advocating for a return to interventionist policies that prioritize national over international economic interests (Tsim, 2025; *Trump's Trade War Is No Bluff*, 2025).

Globalization and Economic Sovereignty

Political debates over globalization underscored the impact of Trump's economic policies on domestic and international markets. By challenging multilateral trade agreements and advocating for bilateral deals prioritizing American interests, the administration sought to restructure global economic relationships.

While this strategy drew support from some quarters as a means of reclaiming economic sovereignty, others viewed it as a retreat from constructive international engagement (Dean, 2025).

National Rhetoric and Cultural Identity

Culturally, Trump's economic policies were framed within a nationalistic rhetoric that combined economic and cultural identities. The language of "America First" resonated with voters who perceived economic debates as part of a broader cultural struggle against liberal elites and globalism. This framing reinforced support among Trump's base, influencing political discourse more broadly and setting the stage for future movements seeking economic reform on nationalist lines (Latham, 2025).

Intersectionality of Economic Policy

Trump's policies also had significant implications for racial and ethnic group responses. While some minority groups remained skeptical of the administration's broader policy agenda, economic strategies focusing on job creation and local industry investment appealed to those prioritizing economic opportunity over other political considerations.

This delicate balance highlighted the intersectionality of economic policy, cultural identity, and political allegiance, reflecting broader shifts in American voter demographics (Edsall, 2024).

Debates on Economic Nationalism and Interventionism

The conversation around economic nationalism during Trump's presidency gave rise to renewed interest in economic policies that prioritized national over global considerations. This shift inevitably prompted discussions about the long-term sustainability of protectionist measures and their effects on the American economy and global trade relations.

As debates on economic nationalism and interventionism continue, the legacy of Trump's economic policies will remain central to shaping future conservative ideologies and political strategies.

Environmental Policies

The topic of environmental policies provides a natural progression in examining how economic and philosophical shifts under various presidencies have influenced contemporary politics. Conjectural debates surrounding environmental policies—a critical area in which economic considerations intersect with political commitments—continue to shape public discourse and mobilization efforts.

As such, understanding the economic and cultural impacts of Trump's presidency provides necessary context for analyzing how environmental policy shifts follow a similar trajectory, heavily influenced by various mandates and the demands of many political constituencies.

Legacy of Economic Nationalism

Trump's economic policies and their framing within the "America First" agenda represented a critical moment in the evolution of conservative thought. The emphasis on protectionism, manufacturing growth, and energy independence introduced a new dimension to conservative economic doctrine, one that prioritizes national interests and challenges the tenets of globalization.

These shifts altered American political ideology and set the groundwork for ongoing debates about the intersection of economic policy, cultural identity, and political allegiance in modern American politics.

Next, we'll investigate shifts in environmental policies, particularly how the Trump presidency altered economic strategies. This change emphasized deregulation, impacting environmental responsibility and prompting debates over market-oriented approaches versus regulatory frameworks, setting the stage for significant political discourse on climate action.

Shifts in Environmental Policies

The Trump presidency ushered in a distinct shift in economic policies, leaving a lasting influence on America's political direction. The hallmark of this administration's economic strategy lay in its reduction of regulatory barriers, aiming to stimulate business growth and boost the overall economy.

This scaling back of regulations extended beyond the financial sector, influencing environmental policymaking and prompting a re-evaluation of the nation's stance on environmental responsibility.

Deregulation and Market-Oriented Environmentalism

The recalibration of economic policies under Trump is in keeping with broader theoretical shifts. His administration's emphasis on deregulation crossed over into the environmental domain, aligning with conservatives' market-oriented visions. This approach favored exploiting natural resources and scaling back protections, positing that economic growth could coexist with environmental stewardship by way of market solutions.

This dogmatic positioning sparked debates over the functionality and ethical implications of entrusting market forces with safeguarding ecological health. The administration's withdrawal from the Paris Agreement demonstrated this pivot, illustrating a significant fracture in consensus over global climate cooperation (Global Markets News Team, 2024).

Regulatory vs. Market-Based Approaches

As we dig deeper into the evolution of environmental policies, the dynamics of contemporary political thoughts and ideas emerge, molded by successive presidencies' varying approaches to climate change and sustainability. The interplay between regulatory and market-based approaches characterizes this evolution, serving as a battleground for philosophical divides.

Under Trump, the regulatory rollback catalyzed a resurgence of market-based environmentalism, which critics argued compromised long-term ecological security for short-term economic gains. These divergences manifested in stark contrasts in policy prescriptions, reflecting the broader sociopolitical schisms (Balsanek et al., 2025).

Climate Adaptation and Resilience

Recent administrations have ridden this wave, refocusing public discourse around climate adaptation and resilience. The push for regulatory frameworks, such as the Green New Deal proposition by progressive politicians, epitomizes this sociopolitical reorientation.

This approach argues that governmental intervention is necessary to steer society toward lower carbon futures, challenging the efficacy of the previous administration's deregulatory stance. The administration's stance often clashed with burgeoning grassroots environmental movements that spotlighted the dire social and ecological consequences of policy negligence (Nisbett & Spaiser, 2023).

Grassroots Movements and Advocacy

Grassroots activism, a vital component of environmental advocacy, has played an instrumental role in reshaping public opinion and influencing political action. Movements spearheaded by influential figures such as Greta Thunberg have captured global attention, underscoring the urgency of taking decisive action against climate change.

These grassroots movements, grounded in collective action, have worked hard to break traditional boundaries and make the most of community mobilization. The fight against industrial pollution and fossil fuels has emerged as emblematic of grassroots environmentalism's impact, influencing political agendas and creating ripple effects in legislative chambers (Kumar, 2024).

Chapter 7 Contemporary Ideological Shifts

Youth Activism and Normative Shifts

The moral momentum generated by youth activists has notably permeated international climate politics, marking a philosophical change. These young leaders stand as norm entrepreneurs, challenging long-established perspectives and wielding moral authority to rally global consciousness around climate justice.

Through digital platforms and social media tools, activists have successfully steered conversations toward prioritizing varied climate justice narratives, elevating previously marginalized voices, and reshaping the dialogue around climate policies. This phenomenon reflects a normative shift that breaks barriers, punctuating the discourse at major international gatherings like the annual UNFCCC conferences (Nisbett & Spaiser, 2023).

Legislative Examples and Conceptual Divides

Examining concrete legislative examples furthers our understanding of the magnitude of these thought-oriented shifts. The Clean Power Plan, introduced during the Obama administration, is a perfect example of regulatory ambitions aimed at curbing carbon emissions from power plants.

Although its implementation faced significant political opposition and was eventually supplanted by less stringent standards under Trump, the plan symbolizes the tug-of-war over the scope and depth of environmental regulations.

Conversely, market-based approaches like cap-and-trade systems offer alternative pathways for curbing emissions through economic incentives. These schemes, while politically contentious, reflect the underpinnings of market-oriented environmental policy frameworks.

Amid these competing visions, the public remains divided, highlighting the persistently fractured political environment that shapes policy outcomes (Alemany, 2017).

Science, Policy, and Public Perception

The complexity of these ideological shifts is further compounded by ongoing scientific discourse. The interdependence between science, policy, and public perception illustrates the particular challenges of driving environmental governance. Policymakers must grapple with rapidly evolving scientific insights and the messy intersection of competing interests and ethical considerations.

These varying opinions and attempts at compromise highlight the delicate nature of environmental advocacy, where science serves as both a guide and a battleground for policy debates (Webb et al., 2020).

Electoral Politics and Environmental Advocacy

Through this lens, electoral politics acts as a stage where environmental advocacy's philosophies and impacts come to light. Candidates increasingly find themselves needing to agree with environmental agendas that resonate with an electorate increasingly sensitive to climate ramifications.

The momentum of grassroots movements and youth activism has wielded a significant influence, reshaping electoral strategies and driving politicians to incorporate climate narratives into campaign platforms. The paradigm shifts within political ideologies highlight the inextricable link between public sentiment and the responsiveness of governance structures.

Chapter 7 Contemporary Ideological Shifts

As a result, contemporary shifts in environmental policies are far from monolithic; they are a complicated mix of grassroots activism, scientific discourse, and evolving political narratives. As these philosophical frameworks continue to evolve, the debates and policies they beget will inevitably affect and reach people in power, reshaping the paradigms by which societies address the existential challenge of climate change.

Concluding Thoughts

Reflecting on the influence of recent presidencies on modern political ideologies reveals distinct impacts on public policy. From George W. Bush's War on Terror to Barack Obama's Affordable Care Act and Donald Trump's trade wars, each administration has waded through complex global challenges and created new political frameworks.

These shifts in national security, health care, and economic policies demonstrate an evolving political thought. Educators, students, and general readers alike can gain insights into how past presidential actions shape today's societal environment and inform future political discourse and engagement.

In the next chapter, we will explore how communication strategies evolved through presidencies from Roosevelt to Obama. Each leader faced unique challenges—including Roosevelt's fireside chats, Nixon's television battles, Clinton's adaptive approach, and Obama's digital engagement. This analysis will highlight the critical role of public communication in shaping public perception and leadership effectiveness.

Chapter 8

Influence of Public Opinion in Leadership

The crackling sound of a radio united families during the Great Depression. As night fell, eager listeners tuned in to hear President Franklin D. Roosevelt speak, his voice soothing and reassuring like a close family member. He conveyed hope, turning complex policies into relatable stories. This connection bridged the gap between the leader and the nation during challenging times.

Public opinion has always significantly influenced presidential actions, and Roosevelt's fireside chats were a means of engaging the nation in conversation. This chapter will explore how public sentiment shapes presidential decisions and the communication strategies leaders use to navigate this powerful force.

Chapter 8 Influence of Public Opinion in Leadership

The Influence of Public Communication Strategies

Franklin D. Roosevelt's fireside chats offered a strategic masterclass in leadership during challenging times. As the Great Depression wore on, Americans needed reassurance and hope. FDR realized this need and turned to radio, then a widespread and trusted medium, to connect directly with the public.

He spoke in a calm, reassuring voice that advanced a sense of personal connection with each listener. It's said that his smooth style made listeners feel as though he was right there in their living rooms, engaging in intimate conversation.

Bridging Policy and Personal Outreach

Roosevelt's ability to pivot from policy to personal outreach during his fireside chats provided a lifeline to citizens facing economic uncertainty. In a time when economic fears gripped the nation, the broadcasts became a symbol of hope and strength. Each address served as a narrative bridge between Roosevelt's policy measures and the lived realities of the American people.

By explaining complex policies in plain language, FDR demystified the often arcane world of government for everyday citizens. This approach was a hallmark of his communication strategy, enabling Roosevelt to turn sophisticated legislative agendas into digestible, relatable narratives (*FDR's Fireside Chat*, 2020).

The New Deal and Public Reassurance

An illustrative example of the power of these chats came during the implementation of the New Deal. Americans, many of whom were grappling with wage cuts, layoffs, and unemployment, needed reassurance that the government had a practical recovery strategy. FDR masterfully used the radio to disclose the essence of the New Deal, framing it not just as a series of legislative acts but also as a personal commitment to national revitalization.

Programs such as the Civilian Conservation Corps (CCC) and the Federal Deposit Insurance Corporation (FDIC) were introduced through these chats, with FDR drawing clear connections between these initiatives and the prosperity they aimed to restore (History.com Editors, 2025g).

Codes of Fair Practice

Through radio, Roosevelt addressed concerns, adapted his messaging, and built a more cohesive national mood of optimism and security. For instance, in a July 1933 broadcast, he discussed the purposes and value of the National Recovery Administration (NRA), explaining how codes of fair practice would stabilize business and create jobs.

His conversational tone made complex economic principles understandable and relevant to ordinary citizens, garnering greater public acceptance and enthusiasm for the initiatives. Interestingly, the NRA's mascot, the Blue Eagle, and the phrase "We do our part" became an emblem of public participation in economic recovery, endorsed heavily in FDR's talks.

This branding pushed the idea that recovery was a collective responsibility, elevating community spirit and national solidarity at a time when both were in short supply. Families across the country displayed the Blue Eagle symbol with pride, reflecting an era where citizens felt directly involved in the nation's economic drive (Terrell, 2025; Bleckman, 2021).

Building Trust and Leadership Confidence

Over time, the immediate trust built through these broadcasts translated into widespread support for FDR's administration. Even as critics emerged, challenging some New Deal policies, the trust these radio talks had earned ensured an unprecedented level of confidence in FDR's leadership.

The Legacy of the Fireside Chats

The fireside chats served as a precedent for future leaders in the art and necessity of public engagement. Roosevelt's strategy demonstrated that when leaders listen to and respect their constituents' concerns, while providing clear and consistent messaging, they bridge gaps in understanding and reinforce their legitimacy.

As we skip forward to the era of President Richard Nixon, it becomes clear that FDR's fireside chats laid foundational communication strategies indispensable to addressing crisis and dissent.

Communication Strategies Across Eras

Nixon, facing anti–Vietnam War protests, encountered a skeptical public with access to new media. His strategies shifted from intimate radio talks to visually driven communications on television, highlighting the need for presidential administrations to heed public sentiment. Nixon's struggles with anti-war sentiment showed that while media evolves, the demand for transparency and direct engagement remains vital.

Navigating Protests and Public Dissent

Franklin D. Roosevelt's fireside chats set a precedent for engaging public sentiment and essentially mobilizing opinion, providing a contrasting backdrop for Nixon's challenges during the Vietnam War. While FDR skillfully addressed the public's mood to nurture support, Nixon grappled with an increasingly critical public questioning U.S. involvement in Vietnam.

As opposition grew, the administration faced a mounting wave of anti-war protests that would drastically shape its policy decisions.

Reluctance to Engage Public Sentiment

The tension between Nixon and public sentiment highlights the reluctance of his administration to initially engage with the widespread discontent over the Vietnam War. This reluctance intensified national divisions and affirmed a critical contrast to earlier administrations that had communicated with the public and, therefore, earned their trust.

Public opinion during the Vietnam War was fraught with complexity, heavily shaped by mass protests, and significantly amplified by the media. These factors placed mounting pressure on Nixon to take public sentiment seriously to maintain control over the political narrative (Forte, 2017).

The Impact of Anti-War Protests

Anti-war protests, particularly in the late 1960s and early 1970s, significantly shaped Nixon's policy decisions. The moratorium to end the war in Vietnam in October 1969 brought hundreds of thousands of protesters to Washington, DC, vividly illustrating the depth of opposition among Americans. Media coverage of such events forced the Nixon administration to confront the reality of this growing dissent.

The administration's strategy initially focused on discrediting protestors and emphasizing party loyalty, prioritizing keeping the silent majority—those who supported the war but were not vocal—in line. However, the scale and persistence of the protests warranted a more strategic response (Levering, 2019).

Vietnamization: A Strategic Concession

Nixon's policy of "Vietnamization" exemplified a strategic concession to public pressure. Announced on November 3, 1969, this policy aimed to reduce American military involvement by transferring more combat responsibilities to South Vietnamese forces. This was an attempt to quell public dissatisfaction and manage the home front's perception of U.S. foreign policy.

He acknowledged the war's divisiveness when addressing the nation, stating the need to win America's peace while signaling a shift in strategy (History.com Editors, 2025e).

The Pentagon Papers and Public Mistrust

The Pentagon Papers significantly impacted Nixon's administration, illustrating further complications arising from public opinion. Published by *The New York Times* in 1971, these documents revealed that successive U.S. administrations had misled the public about Vietnam, deepening mistrust toward the government.

Nixon's reaction to this leak was marked by paranoia and a strong assertion of control, which led to the infamous development of the White House Special Investigations Unit, known as the "Plumbers." These events further exemplified the reactive and sometimes draconian measures that Nixon's presidency resorted to in handling dissent (Moran, 2023).

Balancing Domestic Unrest and Foreign Policy

As disillusionment soared, internal and external pressures grew. Nixon faced the challenge of presenting a front of resolve and control while discreetly negotiating reductions in troop numbers and peace talks to alleviate domestic unrest. The announcement of Vietnamization was an attempt to shift public perception from active warfare to a gradual disengagement that still promised commitment without heavy involvement.

Nixon asserted that immediate withdrawal would be disastrous, maintaining that a steady, organized exit strategy through Vietnamization would secure greater peace and security for future generations.

Despite these efforts, the discontent continued, manifesting in protests that epitomized the American public's growing frustration with the lack of transparency and apparent stall in diplomatic progress. Nixon's subsequent policies and speeches attempted to recapture and reorganize public opinion onto a more favorable trajectory. However, the continuing leak, public protests, and growing demands for accountability fueled

Nixon's determination to tighten control and seek unfettered influence over the narrative (Li, 2024).

Reactive Governance and Public Influence

Nixon's reactive handling of public dissent highlights the relationship between governance and public influence. Nixon's method was largely one of reactivity, a departure from the proactive mobilization of public sentiment exemplified by FDR's fireside chats. This reactivity underscored how Nixon's administration struggled to incorporate evolving public demands into its strategic outlook, instead often doubling down on domestic control and securitization efforts.

Nonetheless, these challenges also emphasized the complexities of presidential engagement with dissent, illustrating the impact of widespread public sentiment on decision-making, especially in times of war. The challenges Nixon faced during the Vietnam War show that responding to public pressure is neither simple nor straightforward but instead a balancing act often fraught with tension and the constant risk of political fallout (Forte, 2017).

Clinton's Communication Strategy

As we transition to discussing President Bill Clinton's presidency, we are reminded of lessons learned during Nixon's tenure. Like Nixon, Clinton maneuvered an era of complex public-relations fraught with scandal and intense media scrutiny. However, Clinton's administration arguably incorporated a more adaptive communication strategy, using modern media to engage more directly and transparently with the public.

Scandal Management and Modern Media Engagement

Public opinion plays an undeniable role in shaping the decisions and communication strategies of U.S. presidents. This relationship is consistent throughout the history of American leadership, visible from Nixon's era to the more recent administrations of Clinton and Obama. Each president dealt with this dynamic differently, illustrating a constantly evolving presidential communication style.

Clinton's Engagement Through Cable News and Digital Platforms

Consider Nixon's efforts to manage public perception during the Vietnam War through carefully written speeches and strategic media appearances. He understood the need to reconcile his public messaging with the sentiments of a war-weary population, thereby utilizing media to bridge gaps between government actions and public opinion.

Similarly, during Clinton's presidency, the landscape of public engagement began to shift with the growing influence of cable news and emerging digital platforms. Clinton's adeptness in connecting with the electorate, reflecting their concerns in his policies, demonstrated an evolution in leadership strategies.

He constructively used town halls and televised addresses to connect with citizens on a personal level, portraying a sense of transparency and relatability that endeared him to many (Vorberg & Zeitler, 2019).

Obama's Digital Revolution

Obama's administration marked a significant turning point in presidential communication, characterized by the adept use of social media and internet platforms to disseminate information. While traditional media maintained its role, the Obama administration utilized more direct avenues for communication through social media.

This digital strategy aimed to control narratives, engage younger audiences, and enhance transparency by providing data directly to the public. However, it faced criticism for being overly controlled, with some journalists feeling sidelined by this shift.

The Obama administration's strategy reflected a balance between openness and control. While statistics showed an increase in interviews with news and digital media, seasoned journalists criticized their methods for limiting press access to critical information. This strategy highlighted a notable shift in leadership, navigating between public engagement and media manipulation to reflect the public's sentiments (Downie & Rafsky, 2013).

The Evolution of Media and Public Engagement

Exploring these examples, one can see how the evolution of media and public engagement reflects a broader narrative: the perennial challenge for presidents to adapt to changing public tastes while maintaining political leverage. The digital era has redefined communication avenues while furthering scrutinized presidential actions. Public opinion, more immediate and influential than ever, requires swift and strategic responses.

Scandals and Strategic Communication

Presidents have often capitalized on crises or scandals to reshape public perception. The Clinton administration, dealing with scandals such as his impeachable conduct, responded with strategic apologies and diversions to reorient the public focus. This reflects a broader pattern: Leaders often adapt their communication tactics amid controversies to standardize public sentiment with political imperatives.

These strategic shifts usually involve heightened media engagement and, at times, a change in policy direction. The email scandal under Hillary Clinton during the 2016 presidential election exemplifies this. The media frenzy and public discourse around this incident massively influenced public perception.

Emergent platforms such as social media played important roles in escalating or mitigating such narratives (Blum, 2017). In handling these controversies, public opinion dictated the need for a new narrative.

The Impact of Scandals on Communication Strategies

Political scandals often require a critical re-evaluation of communication strategies. The rise in scandals can be attributed to increased media scrutiny and a more discerning public. Consequently, leaders must adapt to communicate transparency, realigning the public's perception.

This adaptation is not solely a defensive maneuver but also an opportunity for political redemption. As media proliferation continues, scandals that might have previously remained under wraps now demand full-fledged communication strategies to deal with the complexities of public sentiment successfully.

The always-evolving media has enabled the public to actively partake in these narratives. The widespread use of social media reflects this shift toward participatory communication. The platform serves as both a tool for narrative control and a conduit for democratic engagement.

The relationship between public opinion and presidential decision-making becomes more pronounced when social media amplifies both commendations and criticisms (*Crisis Communication*, 2023).

Public Opinion's Role in Leadership

Public opinion exerts far-reaching influence, compelling leaders to anticipate expectations and adapt strategies. The evolution from traditional media to digital platforms requires a deep understanding of the nuanced role of public sentiment in leadership. Embracing this understanding leads to more productive governance, where presidential actions reflect the public's evolving expectations.

Hence, the historical trajectory from Nixon to modern leaders offers examples of the symbiotic relationship between presidential actions and public opinion, growing more significant with each technological and societal shift. What remains clear is that in an age where information exchange is constant and rapid, leaders must listen and authentically respond to public opinion to sustain their relevance and thereby guide national discourse.

Concluding Thoughts

Presidential actions are closely linked to public sentiment and evolving communication strategies. Franklin D. Roosevelt's fireside chats exemplified direct dialogue with Americans during crises, showing media's role in connecting policy and public understanding. Following Nixon's era, which highlighted challenges in addressing dissent, modern leaders, including Clinton and Obama, adapted to media changes, focusing on transparency and narrative control.

Understanding these shifts allows exploration of communication's impact on trust and policy. Educators and students can discuss governance, accountability, and public sentiment's influence on presidential decisions.

In the next chapter, we will explore how personal convictions shaped presidential actions in American governance, focusing on Jefferson's church-state separation, Lincoln's emancipation beliefs, Carter's moral leadership, and Reagan's conservative revolution.

Chapter 8 Influence of Public Opinion in Leadership

Chapter 9

The Role of Personal Beliefs

While leading a young country, Thomas Jefferson envisioned a democracy where individual belief systems could thrive without state-endorsed religion. He contemplated how a government can ensure liberty if it endorses any faith. His reflections formed the cornerstone of his mission to protect individual rights.

In this chapter, we look into the pivotal role of Thomas Jefferson in establishing the principles of religious freedom and the separation of church and state during his presidency. His Enlightenment ideals influenced governance while shaping the framework for these important rights, seen through his drafting of the Virginia Statute for Religious Freedom.

We will also examine how Lincoln's and Carter's moral convictions further impacted American political history, revealing the deep connection between personal beliefs and leadership.

Chapter 9 The Role of Personal Beliefs

Jefferson and the Separation of Church and State

During Thomas Jefferson's presidency, the societal and political climate was deeply rooted in the Enlightenment ideals that championed reason, scientific inquiry, and individual rights. These principles heavily influenced Jefferson's convictions about governance, particularly in the area of religious freedom and the separation of church and state.

The Enlightenment philosophers, emphasizing natural rights and the power of reason, shaped Jefferson's viewpoint that religion should be separate from government control. This was at a time when the United States was trying to define itself apart from European traditions of state-sponsored religion and monarchy.

Jefferson's presidency coincided with the challenges of incorporating these ideals into the practical workings of a new nation, which was a powerful backdrop for his legislative and philosophical contributions.

The Virginia Statute for Religious Freedom

One critical legislative achievement that encapsulated Jefferson's commitment to these principles was the Virginia Statute for Religious Freedom. Drafted by Jefferson and enacted in 1786, it outlined his vision of religious liberty by affirming that no person should be compelled to attend or support any religious worship or ministry against their belief.

Conversely, the statute particularly emphasized that opinions in the field of religion should not be subjected to the will of the government. This was an influential departure from practices under colonial rule, where dissenters from the established Church of England often faced persecution. The statute's passage marked a foundational moment for religious freedom, framing it as a natural right alongside other liberties.

The significance lay in its direct challenge to the traditional entanglement of ecclesiastical and governmental powers, setting a precedent for the First Amendment protections in the U.S. Constitution (*Thomas Jefferson and the Virginia Statute for Religious Freedom*, n.d.).

Challenges and Controversies

Challenges during his presidency further highlighted the importance of maintaining a clear demarcation between religious and state affairs. One notable controversy was the opposition he faced due to his religious skepticism and belief in deism, a perspective that envisaged God as a distant creator not interfering in worldly affairs.

These beliefs often made Jefferson the target of vicious pamphlets and criticisms branding him an atheist. Yet, Jefferson's consistency in advocating for religious freedom defined his public persona and policies and solidified the principle in American governance (Ragosta, 2018).

Jefferson's Writings and Vision for Secularism

In his extensive letters and writings, Jefferson fervently articulated his vision for a secular state. His correspondence with political contemporaries demonstrates this philosophy, notably declaring to Benjamin Rush his resolve against all forms of tyranny over the mind of man, a sentiment underlining his resistance to religious imposition by the state.

These writings revealed his strategy to direct the divisive political landscape where differing religious factions vied for power and influence. The public reception of his views was mixed, hailing him as a visionary by some and as a subversive figure by others. Nonetheless, his determined advocacy for the separation of church and state reverberated through American political thought, influencing interpretations of religious freedom long after his presidency ended (Boles, 2017).

Long-Term Implications

The long-term implications of Jefferson's beliefs and policies have often been areas of significant historical and scholarly exploration. His commitment to religious freedom has been regarded as setting a critical precedent for subsequent presidential administrations. By championing the separation of church and state as a necessary foundation for a diversified democracy, Jefferson's actions established durable standards for the relationship between religion and government.

This has continued to factor into various Supreme Court decisions and legislative debates about religious expression and its place in public life. Understanding Jefferson's message provides required insights into contemporary discussions about how to balance religious liberty with other societal needs in a constantly evolving culture (Rogers Stevens et al., 2025).

Lincoln's Evolving Views

Presidential leadership under Abraham Lincoln reveals how personal convictions influence significant political decisions. Lincoln's actions toward abolishing slavery reflect evolving beliefs that shaped national policy and identity. His evolving views illustrate how personal beliefs critically influence presidential actions.

While Jefferson's legacy established civil liberties, Lincoln's moral considerations regarding slavery represent a leadership dimension rooted in personal belief and courage, highlighting convictions as vital in shaping American political history.

Presidents' Personal Views

Throughout history, personal beliefs have played an all-important role in shaping leadership, and this was no different for Abraham Lincoln.

Lincoln's Personal Views on Emancipation

Lincoln's evolving convictions about slavery and freedom significantly influenced his presidency. Despite initial resistance and criticism from different quarters, such as the reaction of Kentuckians and the cautious approach of the *New York Herald*, Lincoln's moral commitment to emancipation remained steadfast.

While heavily contested, emancipation was central to his strategy for preserving the Union. Lincoln's correspondence with Albert G. Hodges reveals how his anti-slavery sentiment was tempered by a deep respect for the constitutional limits of the presidency. His thoughtful approach demonstrated that personal beliefs, while influential, had to be balanced with practical and constitutional considerations.

His emphasis on the "indispensable necessity" of emancipation was driven by a blend of moral conviction and strategic necessity (Osmani, 2015).

Chapter 9 The Role of Personal Beliefs

Carter's Emphasis on Moral Leadership

The way personal convictions influence presidential actions shows how deeply rooted beliefs drive significant policy decisions. Carter's presidency serves as a prime example of how a president's personal beliefs—particularly his moral convictions—shaped both his leadership style and policy directives. This section digs into how Carter's upbringing and personal integrity influenced his tenure, anchoring his governance approach in a pronounced dedication to human rights and ethical governance.

Religious Upbringing and Integrity

Jimmy Carter's presidency is a prime example of leadership guided by a deep-rooted moral compass. His religious upbringing played a determining role in shaping his worldview. Carter, a devout Christian, spent years teaching Sunday school, embedding in him a strong sense of personal integrity that became evident throughout his political career (Harman, 2024).

This integrity was more than a private virtue; it was a public ethos that he brought to the national stage upon entering the presidency. His personal belief in the importance of decency and human rights set him apart from his predecessors, who often adhered more strictly to realpolitik.

Leading With Conviction

Strong moral convictions shaped Carter's presidency. Stemming from a devout Baptist tradition, his faith operated as a guide, emphasizing principles of honesty and integrity. These themes infused both his leadership style and policy decisions.

Carter's religious convictions were not merely private matters but influenced his public persona, strengthening a presidency marked by a commitment to ethical governance. His focus on human rights exemplified how personal beliefs could reshape foreign policy. Unlike previous administrations, Carter placed human rights at the forefront, reorienting U.S. relations with several nations to agree with his moral stance.

Challenges of Moral Leadership

This emphasis on human rights did not come without challenges. Carter faced resistance from political allies and global partners who were accustomed to prioritizing strategic interests over moral considerations. Nevertheless, Carter's insistence on moral leadership set a new precedent, demonstrating how deeply held beliefs can inspire policy shifts, albeit with some political costs.

Importantly, this ethical focus extended beyond foreign affairs to domestic policy areas like energy conservation and economic equity. Carter approached these issues with a sense of ethical responsibility, viewing them as moral imperatives rather than mere policy objectives. His administration's push for energy conservation and addressing economic inequality reflected his belief in stewardship and fairness (Gupta, 2024).

Contrasts Between Lincoln and Carter

Carter's leadership contrasted sharply with his predecessors. While Lincoln balanced his personal beliefs with constitutional mandates, Carter's presidency was marked by a direct alignment with his moral convictions. For example, Carter's emphasis on transparency diverged from the more opaque political maneuvers of previous administrations.

This integrity-driven leadership style, however, sometimes led to challenges, as political and moral idealism often clashed. Carter's legacy, however, persists in its demonstration of how integrity can inform leadership, presenting a model that remains relevant in political discussions today.

Carter's Legacy and Reagan's Conservative Revolution

Carter's presidency provides context for understanding subsequent political developments. His vision paved the way for ideological shifts during Reagan's conservative revolution, highlighting the potential of moral leadership while exposing its complexities and limitations. Carter's ethical governance contrasted with the incoming wave of conservatism focused on deregulation.

Nevertheless, his emphasis on human rights and moral responsibility left a lasting impact on presidential ethics. Similarly, Lincoln's commitment to ending slavery reshaped societal norms. Both leaders demonstrated how personal beliefs shape presidential action, influencing ongoing discussions about morality, politics, and leadership in political history (Einhorn et al., 2025).

Human Rights as a Foreign Policy Tenet

A critical aspect of Carter's presidency was his focus on human rights as a central tenet of foreign policy. His goal was to reshape America's international engagements by prioritizing human decency over strategic interests. Carter's commitment to human rights was not just rhetoric; it was a guiding principle, as well. This conviction was revolutionary for U.S. foreign policy, as he sought to distance the nation from the morally ambiguous alliances that defined the Vietnam and Nixon eras. His administration's emphasis on upholding international norms and elevating human rights highlighted a transformative shift in diplomatic approaches (Mann, 2023).

The Camp David Accords

Carter's deep commitment to peace, guided by his moral clarity, led to remarkable achievements, such as the Camp David Accords, where he spearheaded negotiations between Egypt and Israel. This breakthrough agreement paved the way for the first Israeli–Arab peace treaty and signified Carter's tenacity in anchoring diplomacy in ethical responsibility.

The Accords epitomized his belief that moral leadership could render genuine outcomes, even amid political complexities (Carter, 2025).

Domestic Policies Rooted in Ethics

Beyond foreign policy, Carter's ethical convictions also drove domestic policies, notably in energy conservation and social equity. He perceived the energy crisis as an ethical challenge, urging Americans to conserve resources for the collective good and future generations.

His belief in ethical governance propelled him to champion energy-efficient technologies and reduce dependency on foreign oil. Carter's proposals, such as tax credits for renewable-energy initiatives, reflected his commitment to a sustainable future—a presidency hallmark built on an ethical framework (Strong, 2025).

Addressing Social Inequities

Carter's dedication to addressing social inequities also exemplified his moral leadership. He often highlighted the disparity between America's ideals and social realities, advocating for disadvantaged communities. His policies, aimed at reducing economic disparities, personified his commitment to ethical governance.

Initiatives such as the expansion of public health programs and investments in rural development were driven by his belief in fairness and equity (Sonnenfeld, 2025).

Post-Presidential Legacy

The breadth of Carter's moral leadership extends beyond his presidency into his post-presidential work, forming a unique legacy of integrity and civic responsibility. Carter's vision continued through efforts like conflict mediation and promoting global health. His establishment of the Carter Center emphasized his belief in making tangible impacts on society, further solidifying his stature as a moral leader. He set a precedent by using his prestige as a former president to better society and serve humanity.

Carter's legacy as a model of moral responsibility and personal belief in leadership continues to inspire U.S. politics. Future leaders have drawn from his example to ponder the role of ethics in governance. His commitment to moral clarity in policy-making set a benchmark for how presidential convictions can positively shape national and global narratives (Harman, 2024).

The Power of Personal Convictions

As we explore Ronald Reagan's personal beliefs and their impact on American politics, we see a contrasting approach to Jimmy Carter's moral-driven leadership. Reagan's ideologically based agenda brought about a shift in American conservative politics and redefined the politics at the time.

This examination of Carter's presidency illustrates how personal convictions influence leadership styles and policy decisions. The transition from Carter to Reagan reveals a compelling narrative on how personal beliefs—whether moral or ideological—shape presidential legacies and national trajectories.

Reagan's Conservative Revolution

Following the thread of personal convictions shaping presidential actions from the previous focus on Carter, we turn to Reagan, whose personal beliefs sparked a revolution in conservative politics. Reagan's undertaking to conservatism emerged from his shift from a New Deal Democrat to a champion of the conservative movement.

This transformation was molded by witnessing the economic challenges of the 1970s and a commitment to core ideals of individualism and free-market principles. His narrative of "Morning in America" epitomized a vision of national renewal, influenced by his personal ideology and belief in America's potential.

Economic Philosophy and Reaganomics

Reagan's conservative philosophy was not merely an abstraction; it was the backbone of his presidency and the policies he pursued. One of his principal tenets was a staunch advocacy for smaller government intervention in economic affairs, believing that individual initiative and enterprise were key for prosperity.

To this end, Reagan implemented significant tax cuts, believing they would spur economic growth, a theory often referred to as "supply-side economics" or, colloquially, as "Reaganomics." His economic policies included a massive reduction in federal income taxes alongside extensive deregulation efforts intended to free businesses from governmental constraints (Volle, 2024).

These strategies aimed to invigorate the private sector, support economic competition, and combat the inflation and stagnation that plagued the previous decade.

Debates and Outcomes of Fiscal Policies

Reagan's fiscal policies faced significant debate and scrutiny. Critics derided them as "voodoo economics," critiquing the trickle-down promises that didn't always translate into benefits for all socioeconomic levels. Nevertheless, the economic growth seen during his administration, with reduced inflation and significant job creation, indicated to supporters that his approach had merit.

However, these gains were shadowed by exploding national deficits and the burden of a growing national debt, presenting a skewed picture of the results of his implementation of free-market principles (Volle, 2024).

Cold War Ideology and Military Stance

The Cold War context shaped a critical facet of Reagan's presidency and mirrored his fervent personal beliefs against communism. Early in his tenure, he famously labeled the Soviet Union as an "evil empire," reflecting his deep opposition to its ideologies.

So, Reagan's foreign policy was marked by a massive military stance, underpinned by programs like the Strategic Defense Initiative, colloquially known as "Star Wars," which aimed to shield the United States from nuclear threats through advanced technology.

While controversial and heavily criticized for its feasibility and cost, this initiative underscored Reagan's determination to confront Soviet power through strength rather than détente (Editorial Team, 2024).

Diplomatic Engagement and Disarmament

These military postures coexisted with a surprising willingness to negotiate disarmament with Soviet leaders. Despite his combative rhetoric, Reagan's personal conviction in reducing nuclear arms led to important discussions with Mikhail Gorbachev. These culminated in the Intermediate-Range Nuclear Forces Treaty, which reduced the nuclear arsenals of both superpowers and contributed significantly to thawing tensions.

Despite skepticism from many in his administration, these diplomatic efforts revealed a complex relationship between Reagan's ideological steadfastness and his capacity for pragmatic engagement when it dovetailed with his ultimate goal of ending nuclear threat (Leffler, 2018).

Chapter 9 The Role of Personal Beliefs

Redefining Conservative Politics

Reagan's presidency redefined conservative politics during his time, setting the stage for long-term shifts in political correspondence and ideology in America. By combining economic policies with a conservative agenda of social values—less governmental control, strong defense, and repudiation of communism—he attracted various groups, expanding the Republican base, a legacy that persists to this day.

This realignment hinged on the strength and reach of Reagan's communicated vision—a hallmark of his presidency and the affection he received from a substantial portion of the American public, despite controversies like the Iran-Contra affair, which challenged his administration's ethical assurances (Martinez, 2023).

Legacy of Ideological Commitment

Reagan's ability to articulate a resurgent conservative ideology significantly defined late 20th–century politics. His policies influenced Republican agendas and broader American political discourse, merging economic theory, foreign policy, and fervent ideology.

Reagan's vision reshaped American politics, contributing to ongoing debates. His ideological commitment and charisma highlight the connection between personal conviction and public action, showing how deeply held beliefs can shape a nation's future.

Concluding Thoughts

The presidencies of Thomas Jefferson, Abraham Lincoln, Jimmy Carter, and Ronald Reagan highlight the tremendous influence of personal beliefs on American governance. Jefferson's commitment to the separation of church and state laid the foundation for religious liberty, while Lincoln's evolving view on emancipation illustrated his moral conviction in leadership.

Carter's ethical framework redefined foreign policy through a human rights lens. In contrast, Reagan's ideological commitment reshaped conservative politics, promoting deregulation and strong defense. Together, these leaders demonstrate how deeply held beliefs can impact national policy and shape historical narratives.

In the next chapter, we will reflect on the unintended consequences of presidential decisions, exploring how well-meaning policies can misfire and the evolving nature of the executive office.

Chapter 9 The Role of Personal Beliefs

Chapter 10

Presidential Legacies and Lessons

Throughout history, presidents enacted reforms to tackle societal issues, inspired by ideals and public pressure, aimed at eradicating poverty and uplifting morale. However, as these policies have unfolded, some citizens have inadvertently become reliant on empowering programs or faced economic challenges.

This chapter examines how presidential decisions, communication, and executive power have influenced American history, leaving lasting impacts. It reflects on how presidents shape their legacy and how unintended consequences affect public perception and historical interpretation, exploring the lessons learned in leadership.

Chapter 10 Presidential Legacies and Lessons

Unintended Consequences and Rhetoric Influence on Decisions

Presidential decision-making is a complex process in which intentions and outcomes do not always agree. Policy reforms often unfold as well-meant endeavors aiming to reach societal uplift. Yet, unintended consequences frequently mar these reforms, leading to negative societal impacts. Take, for instance, Lyndon B. Johnson's Great Society, which aimed at eliminating poverty and racial injustice.

While it brought major advancements in civil rights and social safety nets, some of its programs inadvertently created dependencies that stifled upward mobility. This serves as a reminder of the critical need for consequential thinking in policy formulation to avoid opposition and backlash and verify that reforms are sustainable and holistic.

War Decisions and Long-Term Effects

War decisions often arise under the sudden need to protect national interests. However, the full impact of such decisions might not reveal themselves until later. For example, when analyzing military interventions, the Vietnam War emerges as a compelling case study. Initially driven by the aim to curb the spread of communism, it eventually contributed to a reshaping of American national identity, creating deep divisions in the country.

The infamous Gulf of Tonkin Resolution granted expansive war powers without full consideration of long-term effects, leading to protracted conflict and influencing foreign relations for decades. It shows how decisions taken in the throes of immediate crises can lead to lasting instability (The Editors of Encyclopaedia Britannica, 2024c).

Economic Measures and Systemic Challenges

In terms of economic measures, the pursuit of short-term gains can overshadow deeper systemic issues. Policies geared toward quick economic growth sometimes fail to consider long-term implications. An example is the deregulation trend of the 1980s, intending to stimulate market efficiency. While it spurred significant economic activity, it also set the stage for financial crimes and economic disparity.

This points to the need for policies that balance immediate benefits with sustainable, equitable outcomes. Notably, job-creation initiatives often center on quick wins, but such approaches can yield unsustainable industry cycles, leaving sectors vulnerable when consumer trends shift or technology evolves (Geisst, 1993).

Social Interventions and Community Divides

Social issue interventions also reveal the intricacies of presidential decisions. For instance, the federally mandated busing policies intended to desegregate schools in the 1970s aimed to expedite racial equality. Yet, the abrupt, top-down nature of their implementation inadvertently created community divides, leading to resistance and socio-political turmoil (Kennedy, 2025).

Communities found themselves grappling with forced transitions rather than the gradual inclusivity that might have been nurtured through more participative dialogue. The importance of creating such policies through inclusive, community-based discussions becomes apparent, reducing the possibility of polarized outcomes and ensuring the communities' buy-in.

Communication's Far-Reaching Influence

Discourse has wielded far-reaching influence beyond intentions. In the orbit of political discourse, certain speeches have left permanent marks on public sentiment and policy. Franklin D. Roosevelt's Fireside Chats serve as a landmark. These informal addresses utilized radio to encourage a personal connection with the public, steering national morale amid economic turmoil and wartime anxiety (Prasch, 2011).

It demonstrates how presidential messaging can shape expectations and perceptions, laying the groundwork for precedent-setting policy initiatives and influencing subsequent administrations. Accordingly, these speeches become defining moments not merely of personal charisma but of long-lasting impact on national identity and governance philosophies.

Expansion of Executive Power

Connecting unforeseen outcomes to the evolving role of the presidency reveals a vital shift in executive power, often triggered by war or economic crises. This expansion of power, seen through executive orders and national emergencies, blurs the constitutional separation of government branches. The presidency's assertiveness in policy shapes historical interpretations and fuels debates over constitutional changes.

As we explore this expanded role, we must consider how unintended consequences inform evaluations of presidential efficacy. The evolution of presidential authority reflects adaptation to a complex global landscape, impacting legacy, public trust, and governance, defining the frameworks for understanding presidential legacies.

The Evolution of the Executive Office and Historical Interpretation

Understanding the complexities of presidential decisions sets the stage for exploring the significant development of executive power in American history. Over time, this change has been significantly shaped by constitutional amendments, a gradual expansion of power, shifting public expectations, and the global environment. Each shift marks a consequential imprint on the legacy and interpretation of the presidency.

Shaping Presidential Power Through Constitutional Changes

Constitutional changes have laid much of the groundwork for the evolving role of the presidency. Initially, the Constitution offered a skeletal framework of presidential power, with the balance of power heavily laden toward Congress. Over time, several amendments and their interpretations have notably shifted this power distribution.

For instance, the 12th Amendment refined the electoral process, effectively altering political strategies. The 22nd Amendment limited presidential terms, responding to concerns about prolonged power after Franklin Roosevelt's four-term presidency (Peterson, 2019). Also, the interpretative role of the Supreme Court has been influential. Court rulings have often expanded or redefined executive power, as seen in the case of

Chapter 10 Presidential Legacies and Lessons

United States v. Curtiss-Wright Export Corp., which upheld broad presidential discretion in foreign affairs.

These decisions reflect changing societal views and establish new precedents that redefine what presidential authority could entail. It is through these lenses that presidential legacies are evaluated, as amendments and interpretations adapt to societal needs while reconfiguring power dynamics.

Expansion of Presidential Authority

Expansion of presidential power over the decades affirms complicated narrative layers that shape the executive branch's role today. While the framers designed checks and balances to prevent monarchical power, successive presidents have, through crises and legislation, extended their reach.

Abraham Lincoln's suspension of habeas corpus during the Civil War exemplifies an assertive exertion of power under crisis (*Origins of the Modern American Presidency*, 2020). Franklin D. Roosevelt further expanded executive reach through New Deal policies, resulting in the formation of numerous administrative bodies.

Notably, crises have often resulted in amplifying presidential authority. The post-9/11 era witnessed the George W. Bush administration expanding executive power through measures like the Patriot Act, which increased surveillance capabilities. Critics argue such expansions pose threats to civil liberties, yet they reveal the persistent tug-of-war inherent in power debates.

Public Expectations and Media Influence

As the executives' power has grown, so have public expectations. Initially viewed primarily as figureheads, modern presidents must now express national leadership, demonstrating both accountability and transparency. This transition is often influenced by public and media interactions that shape the presidential narrative. For instance, John F. Kennedy's mastery of television redefined presidential image, while Franklin D. Roosevelt's Fireside Chats furthered direct communication with the public.

The media undeniably plays a significant role in sculpting a presidential image, often building narratives that can advance or diminish public trust and authority. Transparency, once a demand for honest leadership, has become an expectation for presidents to handle challenges publicly and candidly (Suciu, 2024).

As historical interpretations of presidential actions ebb and flow, media involvement ensures that these narratives extend beyond domestic borders, intertwining with international perceptions of U.S. leadership.

The Presidency in a Global Context

Global shifts have redefined the presidency, transforming it from a domestic guardian to a global statesperson. Early isolationist policies gave way to increased foreign policy responsibilities post–World War II, with the United States emerging as a dominant global power. This shift required presidents to adeptly manage diplomatic and military roles, shaping international relations.

Globalization has introduced challenges that mandate agile presidential leadership, as exemplified by initiatives addressing climate change, international trade tensions, and global conflicts. These responsibilities have broadened the presidential role, underpinning the necessity for informed diplomacy and strategic conflict resolution (Horowitz, 2004).

Such commitments reflect domestic expectations for proactive presidential engagement in global affairs, with international perceptions of American leadership deeply influenced by these efforts.

Melding Domestic and Global Expectations

The presidency emerges as an increasingly complex institution shaped by constitutional amendments, executive power, public expectations, and global responsibilities. These elements combine to create a governing force accountable to citizens and influential globally. To explore the impact of presidential discourse and public memory on shaping legacies, we need to contextualize modern executive power historically.

This understanding allows for a deeper appreciation of how legacies are created through decisions and narratives that follow a presidency. Recognizing this evolving power narrative prepares us to examine how messaging and memory impact presidential legacies.

Rhetoric and Public Memory Influences on Legacy

Evolving presidential responsibilities highlight the consequential role of communication in shaping leaders' legacies, setting the stage for examining how public memory influences historical perception. Presidential language serves as a foundation in defining leadership, particularly during national crises.

For instance, speeches during times of war or economic hardship have the power to stimulate unity or increase division. The eloquence and tone of these speeches can establish a leader's legitimacy and credibility, as seen when Franklin D. Roosevelt delivered his first inaugural address during the Great Depression.

His assurance and call to "action, and action now" resonated deeply with a nation in distress, demonstrating communication's potential to inspire hope (*Franklin D. Roosevelt*, n.d.).

Messaging During National Crises

In times of crisis, the ability to communicate efficiently can become a defining feature of a presidency. For example, the stirring words of Reagan following the *Challenger* disaster reflect the importance of presidential messaging in times of national grief. Reagan's address didn't just mourn the loss; it reframed the tragedy through the lens of courage and exploration, reflected in his closing reference to the poem "High Flight."

Such speeches embed themselves in public memory and often invite reinterpretation as societal values evolve (Bostdorff & Goldzwig, 2005).

Campaign Discourse and Public Expectations

Beyond crises, campaign language significantly influences legacies by setting public expectations. When candidates make promises, they commit themselves to a vision of governance that the public expects them to fulfill. Take, for example, the New Deal: Roosevelt's promise to provide relief, recovery, and reform established clear benchmarks against which his administration would be judged.

However, discrepancies between campaign language and subsequent policies can undermine public trust. Evaluating the promises of recent administrations shows us the gap often seen between aspirational messaging and the pragmatics of governance (Maurantonio, 2014).

Communication and Public Trust

Presidential communication plays a substantial role in maintaining or eroding public trust. It offers a lens through which the public measures authenticity and accountability, as seen in cases where promises outpace achievements. This phenomenon is especially prevalent when candidates propose sweeping changes during campaigns that become diluted once they confront the realities of governance.

By evaluating these tensions, we can better understand the complex relationship between language and trust, especially in contemporary politics where promises must correspond closely with policies to sustain credibility (Rottinghaus, 2006).

Social Media's Role in Presidential Communication

In politics today, social media has become an indispensable tool for presidential communication. The immediacy and reach offered by platforms like X and Facebook have transformed how messages are written and perceived. Presidents now live in a time when every public utterance can be instantaneously disseminated and critiqued.

This evolution emphasizes the need for mindful communication; leaders must carefully consider tone and substance in their messages to avoid misinterpretations that can escalate into significant challenges. Through the ever-more-interconnected world enabled by social media, presidents have the opportunity—and responsibility—to engage directly with the public. However, this presents the risk of compounding polarization if communication is not carefully managed.

An example of the repercussions of unguarded messaging can be seen in the rise of aggressive online discourse, which underscores the importance of advancing constructive dialogue that encourages unity rather than division. The ability to steer conversations and reactions on these platforms has massive implications for presidential reputations and legacies (Liu, 2022).

Historiography and Evolving Narratives

Presidential actions and narratives do not exist in isolation; they are subject to the interpretation and reinterpretation by historians, commentators, and the public. Understanding historiography is important for analyzing how narratives about presidencies evolve.

Different perspectives on controversial presidencies, for instance, illustrate the mutable nature of public perception. As historians explore archival records, speeches, and policy outcomes, the narratives they construct reflect both the context of the times and the prevailing societal values, demonstrating the fluidity of historical interpretation (Murphy, 2008).

Cultural Manifestations of Presidential Legacies

In exploring how presidential legacies manifest culturally, we see their influence in art, media, and education. Presidential portrayals in films, literature, and the arts reflect societal perceptions and critiques, often serving as a mirror to contemporary values and norms. Such cultural artifacts can also reinforce or challenge the prevailing political narratives, making presidential legacies a fertile ground for interpretation and debate.

A striking example lies in how different periods have portrayed figures like Abraham Lincoln—as the Great Emancipator or a flawed leader. This duality proves how cultural contexts shape narratives around presidential legacies (Cullinane & Ellis, 2018).

Educational Framing

In educational settings, how history frames presidents can significantly influence societal understanding. Textbooks and academic discourse reiterate certain narratives, adding them to the collective consciousness. Educators and historians who re-examine and reinterpret past presidencies provide a mechanism for understanding the complexities and legacies that define them.

This continuous re-evaluation ensures that historical narratives remain relevant, capturing the evolving nature of societal progress and values (Baptiste & Sanchez, 2004).

Shaping Legacies

The power of presidential messaging and public memory affirms its vital role in shaping legacies. By examining speech strategies during crises, scrutinizing campaign discourse against actual policies, and considering the influence of social media, we gain deeper insights into the complicated relationship between language and leadership.

Simultaneously, historiography and cultural manifestations reveal how these elements influence our understanding of presidencies, offering an extensive view of how communication and public memory shape the leaders who define our history.

Concluding Thoughts

Presidential leadership greatly influences governance long after their terms. As educators and students examine these narratives, they learn about decision-making complexities, the ripple effects of messaging, and evolving power structures in government. By studying how past leaders navigated crises and enacted policies, we gain insights into the balance between intention and outcome, clearly showing the need for thoughtful reforms.

These reflections encourage critical discussions about contemporary leadership, allowing future generations to understand shifting political landscapes and gain an appreciation of presidential roles and responsibilities in shaping our world.

As we reach the end of our exploration into presidential leadership, it's clear that governance is a complex journey. Presidents must navigate a labyrinth of personal beliefs, public expectations, and political realities. Every decision they make affects history, influencing future administrations and shaping our understanding of leadership's endless challenges.

This examination calls us to reflect on how past legacies guide current governance and inspire future leaders to embrace adaptability and wisdom in addressing contemporary issues.

Chapter 10 Presidential Legacies and Lessons

Conclusion

As we conclude our exploration into presidential leadership, it becomes apparent that the path to governance is anything but straightforward. The role of a president is a complicated framework built with personal convictions, public opinion, and political necessities. While at the helm, presidents are often faced with daunting challenges that demand a careful balancing act between their deeply held beliefs and the myriad expectations placed upon them by society.

This duality demonstrates a critical truth: Decision-making at the highest level of government is rarely simplistic. Presidents must handle an ever-shifting political environment, making choices that require them to weigh their core values against both short-term demands and long-term consequences. This delicate balance illustrates the depth of complexity inherent in leadership roles, where every decision carries the weight of potential legacy.

The actions of any administration shape immediate governance while casting long shadows over future administrations. Every

Conclusion

policy enacted becomes a chapter in the ongoing narrative of history, offering valuable lessons for those who follow.

It is in this historical context that we consider the deep impact of presidential legacies. These legacies are not merely static elements of history but dynamic forces that continue to shape modern governance. They remind us that while specific policies may evolve or become obsolete, the principles and struggles behind them remain relevant through time.

As we study these legacies, we're compelled to reflect on how past decisions inform present challenges and anticipate future directions. A critical aspect of understanding presidential influence lies in examining the interaction between personal beliefs and societal expectations. Presidents are uniquely positioned to shape national discourse by articulating their values and vision clearly.

When these coincide with public sentiment, they can galvanize support and nurture unity. Conversely, when there is a disconnect between a leader's convictions and the prevailing mood of the populace, tensions arise that can lead to great shifts in policy or even political realignment.

This dynamic illustrates the power inherent in clear communication and strategic correspondence with public opinion. It spotlights the delicate balance leaders must strike between embracing pragmatism and staying true to their ideological compass. Such scenarios provide invaluable case studies for students and educators alike, offering a window into the complexities of leadership beyond academic theory.

Further supplementing this discussion is the evolution of governance itself. Over the years, the presidency has transformed in response to societal changes and external pressures, yet its core responsibility remains constant: guiding the nation through a constantly changing world. This adaptability highlights the necessity for flexibility in leadership, urging contemporary leaders to adopt innovative approaches while respecting foundational principles.

As we close this examination of presidential leadership, several reflective questions naturally arise. How do we, as a society, evaluate a president's success? Is it solely through legislative achievements, or do we consider broader societal impacts? What role does efficient communication play in achieving and sustaining public trust?

And, most importantly, how can future leaders draw from historical lessons to deal with the inherent complexities of governance with wisdom and foresight? In considering these questions, educators, students, and general readers alike are encouraged to engage in deeper discussions about the nature of leadership and its lasting impact on society.

Understanding historical precedents offers pathways to developing informed perspectives on contemporary challenges, contributing to a dialogue that strengthens our collective comprehension of democracy. Through this lens, we gain knowledge of past presidencies and a clearer view of how leadership continues to shape the world in which we live.

Conclusion

References

Admin. (2025, February 18). *Taft's approach to antitrust: A legal perspective*. Lagunabeachcanow. https://lagunabeachcanow.com/tafts-approach-to-antitrust-a-legal-perspective/

Adriaenssens, T. C. (2018). *The 1820s revisited: The Monroe Doctrine through European eyes*. https://www.academia.edu/44836298/The_1820s_Revisited_the_Monroe_Doctrine_through_European_Eyes

Agricultural Adjustment Act: Purpose, impact, and historical context. (2024, April 27). Forever Farms. https://foreverfarms.org/agricultural-adjustment-act/

Aiken, J. R., Salmon, E. D. & Hanges, P. J. (2013). The origins and legacy of the Civil Rights Act of 1964. *Journal of Business and Psychology, 28*(4), 383–399. https://doi.org/10.1007/s10869-013-9291-z

Alemany, J. (2017, March 28). *Trump signs executive order dismantling Obama environmental regulations*. CBS News. https://www.cbsnews.com/news/trump-signs-executive-order-dismantling-obama-environmental-regulations/

Alien and Sedition Acts (1798). (2023, July 27). National Archives. https://www.archives.gov/milestone-documents/alien-and-sedition-acts

The Alien and Seditions Act. (2017, November 17). PBS; American Experience. https://www.pbs.org/wgbh/americanexperience/features/adams-alien-and-seditions-act/

Alliance for Progress (Alianza para el Progreso). (2021, December 15). John F. Kennedy Presidential Library and Museum. https://www.jfklibrary.org/learn/about-jfk/jfk-in-history/alliance-for-progress

Ambar, S. (2023, August 28). *Woodrow Wilson: Impact and legacy*. Miller Center. https://millercenter.org/president/wilson/impact-and-legacy

Andrew Johnson. (2024, January 9). National Park Service. https://www.nps.gov/anjo/andrew-johnson-and-reconstruction.htm

Arnold, P. E. (2025, January 29). *William Taft: Domestic Affairs*. Miller Center. https://millercenter.org/president/taft/domestic-affairs

Balsanek, K., Keyes, G., Gigounas, G., Shirodkar, S., Goodlett, B. & Gebrekirstos, S. (2025, March 28). *Horizon - ESG regulatory news and trends*. DLA Piper. https://www.dlapiper.com/en-za/insights/publications/horizon/2025/horizon-esg-regulatory-news-and-trends-march-2025

Baptiste, H. P. & Sanchez, R. (2004). American presidents and their attitudes, beliefs, and actions surrounding education and multiculturalism. In *Educational Policy* (pp. 33–40). New Mexico State University. https://files.eric.ed.gov/fulltext/EJ781910.pdf

Beaubouef, B. A. (2023). *Clayton Antitrust Act*. EBSCO Information Services. https://www.ebsco.com/research-starters/history/clayton-antitrust-act

Bennett, H. (n.d.). *Kennedy, Johnson, and the Civil Rights Movement*. United States History II; Lumen. https://courses.lumenlearning.com/wm-ushistory2/chapter/kennedy-johnson-and-the-beginning-of-the-civil-rights-movement/

Bergmann, E. (2025). The strategic exploitation of conspiracy theories by populist leaders. *Genealogy*, *9*(2), 41–41. https://doi.org/10.3390/genealogy9020041

Berinsky, A. J. (2015). Rumors and health care reform: Experiments in political misinformation. *British Journal of Political Science*, *47*(2), 241–262. https://doi.org/10.1017/s0007123415000186

Biser, M. (2016, August 19). *The fireside chats: Roosevelt's radio talks*. The White House Historical Association. https://www.whitehousehistory.org/the-fireside-chats-roosevelts-radio-talks

Bittlingmayer, G. (2011). Antitrust and Business Activity: The First Quarter Century. *Business History Review*, *70*(3), 363–401. https://doi.org/10.2307/3117242

Black, J. (2018, February 20). *Eisenhower and the Cold War*. Foreign Policy Research Institute. https://www.fpri.org/article/2018/02/eisenhower-cold-war/

Bleckman, S. (2021, June 2). *We do our part*. Living New Deal. https://livingnewdeal.org/we-do-our-part/

Blum, B. (2017, February 10). *Could a President Hillary Clinton be impeached over her e-mails?* HuffPost. https://www.huffpost.com/entry/could-a-president-hillary_b_9196502

Boles, J. B. (2017). *The Founder's secular vision.* Virginia Magazine. https://uvamagazine.org/articles/the_founders_secular_vision

Bostdorff, D. M. & Goldzwig, S. R. (2005). History, collective memory, and the appropriation of Martin Luther King, Jr.: Reagan's rhetorical legacy. *Presidential Studies Quarterly*, *35*(4), 661–690. https://www.jstor.org/stable/27552723

Braik, F. (2018). New Deal for minorities during the Great Depression. *Journal of Political Science and International Relations*, *1*(1), 20–24. https://doi.org/10.11648/j.jpsir.20180101.13

Bushong, W. (2012). *The life and presidency of William Howard Taft.* The White House Historical Association. https://www.whitehousehistory.org/the-life-and-presidency-of-william-howard-taft

Campbell, A. L. & Shore-Sheppard, L. (2020). The social, political, and economic effects of the Affordable Care Act: Introduction to the issue. *RSF: The Russell Sage Foundation Journal of the Social Sciences*, *6*(2), 1–40. https://doi.org/10.7758/rsf.2020.6.2.01

Capka, J. R. (2006, June 27). *Celebrating 50 years: The Eisenhower Interstate Highway System.* US Department of Transportation. https://www.transportation.gov/testimony/celebrating-50-years-eisenhower-interstate-highway-system

Carter, J. (2025). Camp David Accords. In *Britannica*. https://www.britannica.com/event/Camp-David-Accords

Casper, S. E. (2022, September 22). *Jefferson and the Louisiana Purchase*. America in Class. https://americainclass.org/jefferson-and-the-louisiana-purchase/

Chen, J. (2024, August 5). *1913 Federal Reserve Act: Definition and why it's important*. Investopedia. https://www.investopedia.com/terms/f/1913-federal-reserve-act.asp

Chervinsky, L. M. (2025, January 28). *George Washington: Foreign affairs*. Miller Center; University of Virginia. https://millercenter.org/president/washington/foreign-affairs

Chivvis, C. S., Kavanagh, J., Lauji, S., Malle, A., Orloff, S., Wertheim, S. & Wilcox, R. (2024, July 23). *How can U.S. foreign policy change?* Carnegie Endowment for International Peace. https://carnegieendowment.org/research/2024/07/strategic-change-us-foreign-policy

Cívico, J. C. P. (2025, March 13). *Trump protectionism and tariffs: A threat to globalisation, or to democracy itself?* The Conversation. https://theconversation.com/trump-protectionism-and-tariffs-a-threat-to-globalisation-or-to-democracy-itself-252072

Cohen, R. (1982). Human rights diplomacy: The Carter administration and the Southern Cone. *Human Rights Quarterly*, 4(2), 212–242. https://doi.org/10.2307/762130

Cooper, J. M. (2025). The Square Deal of Theodore Roosevelt. In *Britannica*. https://www.britannica.com/biography/Theodore-Roosevelt/The-Square-Deal

Cox, W. & Love, J. (1996, June). *40 years of the US interstate highway system: An analysis.* Public Purpose. https://www.publicpurpose.com/freeway1.htm

Coyne, R. (2024, September 25). *Watergate experts discuss the Nixon Pardon and presidential power.* Gerald R. Ford School of Public Policy. https://fordschool.umich.edu/news/2024/watergate-experts-discuss-nixon-pardon-and-presidential-power

Crisis communication: Responding effectively to scandals and controversies. (2023, October 5). School of Politics. https://theschoolofpolitics.com/blog/crisis-communication-responding-effectively-to-scandals-and-controversies/

Cullinane, M. & Ellis, S. (2018). *Constructing presidential legacy*. University of Roehampton Research Explorer; Edinburgh University Press. https://pure.roehampton.ac.uk/portal/en/publications/constructing-presidential-legacy

Curren, R. (2020). Patriotism, populism, and reactionary politics since 9.11. *Handbook of Patriotism*. https://doi.org/10.1007/978-3-319-54484-7_8

Current, R. N. (2025). Leadership in war of Abraham Lincoln. In *Britannica*. https://www.britannica.com/biography/Abraham-Lincoln/Leadership-in-war

Daalder, I. H. (2024, August 20). *Decision to intervene: How the war in Bosnia ended.* Brookings. https://www.brookings.edu/articles/decision-to-intervene-how-the-war-in-bosnia-ended/

Davenport, D. & Lloyd, G. (2019, May 6). *The rise of the war metaphor in public policy.* Hoover Institution. https://www.hoover.org/research/rise-war-metaphor-public-policy

Dean, A. (2025, January 20). *Trump, geopolitics and the future of globalisation.* Economist Education. https://www.education.economist.com/insights/viewpoint/trump-geopolitics-and-the-future-of-globalisation

Dobson, A. P. (2005). The Reagan administration, economic warfare, and starting to close down the Cold War. *Diplomatic History, 29*(3), 531–556. https://www.jstor.org/stable/24915133

Donnelly, R. C. (2024, December 29). *Jimmy Carter: His human rights focus helped dismantle the Soviet Union.* Inquirer. https://usa.inquirer.net/162990/jimmy-carter-his-human-rights-focus-helped-dismantle-the-soviet-union

Downie, L. & Rafsky, S. (2013, October 10). *The Obama administration and the press.* Committee to Protect Journalists. https://cpj.org/reports/2013/10/obama-and-the-press-us-leaks-surveillance-post-911/

Eder, M. (2021, October 1). *Lincoln as strategist: Exercising the elements of national power.* War Room. https://warroom.armywarcollege.edu/articles/lincoln-as-strategist/

Edicts Editorial Staff. (2024, March 2). *Constitutional law and national security: Balancing rights and safety.* Edicts Blog. https://edicts.blog/constitutional-law-and-national-security/

Editorial Team. (2024, July 5). *Analyzing Reagan's military policies: Strategies and impacts.* Total Military Insight. https://totalmilitaryinsight.com/reagans-military-policies/

The Editors of Encyclopaedia Britannica. (2007). New Freedom. In *Britannica.* https://www.britannica.com/topic/New-Freedom

The Editors of Encyclopaedia Britannica. (2020a). New Frontier. In *Britannica.* https://www.britannica.com/topic/New-Frontier

The Editors of Encyclopaedia Britannica. (2020b). Virginia and Kentucky Resolutions. In *Britannica.* https://www.britannica.com/event/Virginia-and-Kentucky-Resolutions

The Editors of Encyclopaedia Britannica. (2024a). Black Codes. In *Britannica.* https://www.britannica.com/topic/Black-Codes

The Editors of Encyclopaedia Britannica. (2024b). Era of Good Feelings. In *Britannica.* https://www.britannica.com/event/Era-of-Good-Feelings

The Editors of Encyclopaedia Britannica. (2024c). Gulf of Tonkin Resolution. In *Britannica.* https://www.britannica.com/event/Gulf-of-Tonkin-Resolution

The Editors of Encyclopaedia Britannica. (2025a). How did the Louisiana Purchase affect Native American peoples? In *Britannica*. https://www.britannica.com/question/How-did-the-Louisiana-Purchase-affect-Native-American-peoples

The Editors of Encyclopaedia Britannica. (2025b). Monroe Doctrine. In *Britannica*. https://www.britannica.com/event/Monroe-Doctrine

The Editors of Encyclopaedia Britannica. (2025c). New Deal. In *Britannica*. https://www.britannica.com/event/New-Deal

The Editors of Encyclopaedia Britannica. (2025d). Relations with the Soviet Union of Ronald Reagan. In *Britannica*. https://www.britannica.com/biography/Ronald-Reagan/Relations-with-the-Soviet-Union

The Editors of Encyclopaedia Britannica. (2025e). Strategic Defense Initiative. In *Britannica*. https://www.britannica.com/topic/Strategic-Defense-Initiative

The Editors of Encyclopaedia Britannica. (2025f). Worcester v. Georgia. In *Britannica*. https://www.britannica.com/topic/Worcester-v-Georgia

Edsall, T. B. (2024, July 24). What the Trump-Vance alliance means for the Republican Party. *The New York Times*. https://www.nytimes.com/2024/07/24/opinion/trump-vance-republicans-populism.html

Einhorn, R., Madan, T., Maloney, S., O'Hanlon, M. E., Piccone, T., Rabinovich, I., Riedel, B., Stent, A. & Telhami, S. (2025, January 8). *The legacy of President Jimmy Carter.* Brookings. https://www.brookings.edu/articles/the-legacy-of-president-jimmy-carter/

Eisenhower's highways: Built for defense, not just road trips. (2024, December 17). American Patriot Club. https://americanpatriotclub.com/eisenhowers-highways-built-for-defense-not-just-road-trips/

Erath, J. (2015, April 1). *Union success in the Civil War and lessons for strategic leaders.* National Defense University Press. https://ndupress.ndu.edu/Media/News/Article/581883/union-success-in-the-civil-war-and-lessons-for-strategic-leaders/

Eschner, K. (2017, June 29). *Three ways the interstate system changed America.* Smithsonian Magazine. https://www.smithsonianmag.com/smart-news/three-ways-interstate-system-changed-america-180963815/

Examining Lincoln's views on African Americans and slavery. (2020). Abraham Lincoln Presidential Library and Museum. https://presidentlincoln.illinois.gov/education/educator-resources/teaching-guides/lincolns-views-african-american-slavery/

Exploring the history of the interstate system: Its impact on American life and infrastructure. (2024, November 2). Cars Trucks Roads. https://carstrucksroads.com/history-of-the-interstate-system/

FDR's fireside chat on the Recovery Program. (2020, June 1). National Archives. https://www.archives.gov/education/lessons/fdr-fireside

Fischer, B. (2010). US foreign policy under Reagan and Bush. *Cambridge University Press EBooks*, 267–288. https://doi.org/10.1017/chol9780521837217.014

Forte, T. (2017, April 19). *The Vietnam War and the shifting tides of public opinion | History 118: US History Since 1877*. History 118: US History since 1877; Dickinson College. https://blogs.dickinson.edu/hist-118pinsker/2017/04/19/2895/

Franklin D. Roosevelt: Inaugural address. (n.d.). The American Presidency Project. https://www.presidency.ucsb.edu/documents/inaugural-address-8

Freidel, F. & Sidey, H. (2015, March 15). *Lyndon B. Johnson*. The White House. https://obamawhitehouse.archives.gov/1600/presidents/lyndonbjohnson

Geisst, C. R. (1993). Deregulation and change in the 1980s. *A Guide to Financial Institutions*, 127–147. https://doi.org/10.1057/9780230379077_8

George H. W. Bush - Key events. (2023, August 28). Miller Center. https://millercenter.org/president/george-h-w-bush/key-events

Ginsburg, D. H. (2021). Balancing unquantified harms and benefits in antitrust cases under the consumer welfare standard. *SSRN Electronic Journal*, 3. https://doi.org/10.2139/ssrn.3844831

Gittinger, T. & Fisher, A. (2023, February 6). LBJ champions the Civil Rights Act of 1964. *Prologue Magazine*, 36(2). National Archives. https://www.archives.gov/publications/prologue/2004/summer/civil-rights-act

Global Markets News Team. (2024, December 27). *Trump's deregulation agenda for 2025: Key sectors, opportunities, and risks*. Global Market News. https://globalmarketnews.com/trumps-deregulation-agenda-for-2025-key-sectors-opportunities-and-risks/

Gonyea, D. (2013, July 14). The Civil Rights stand of a young Gerald Ford. NPR. https://www.npr.org/2013/07/14/201946977/the-civil-rights-stand-of-a-young-gerald-ford

Gould, L. L. & Mooney, R. O. (2023). *Theodore Roosevelt becomes U.S. president*. EBSCO Information Services. https://www.ebsco.com/research-starters/history/theodore-roosevelt-becomes-us-president

Greenspan, J. (2025, February 28). *The origins of the presidential cabinet*. History. https://www.history.com/articles/history-of-the-presidential-cabinet

Gupta, P. (2024, December 31). *Jimmy Carter: Leadership, human rights advocacy, and his lasting global impact*. The Invisible Narad. https://theinvisiblenarad.com/jimmy-carter/

Hahn, D. F. & Morlando, A. (1979). A Burkean analysis of Lincoln's second Inaugural Address. *Presidential Studies Quarterly*, *9*(4), 376–379. JSTOR. https://doi.org/10.2307/27547509

Hald-Mortensen, C. (2007, May 2). *John F. Kennedy—Leadership qualities that moved a nation*. ResearchGate. https://www.researchgate.net/publication/277101994_John_F_Kennedy_-Leadership_Qualities_That_Moved_A_Nation

Harman, J. (2024, December 30). *Jimmy Carter's global legacy was moral clarity*. Time. https://time.com/6994984/jimmy-carter-legacy-moral-clarity/

Harris, B. H. (2016). *The Affordable Care Act: An analysis of healthcare access in the United States*. https://repository.arizona.edu/bitstream/handle/10150/612990/azu_etd_mr_2016_0096_sip1_m.pdf?sequence=1

Heakal, R. (2024, January 25). *Glass-Steagall Act of 1933: Definition, effects, and repeal*. Investopedia. https://www.investopedia.com/articles/03/071603.asp

Hill, K. J. (2020). *Balancing national security and the constitution: The security blanket over civil liberties*. Johns Hopkins University. https://jscholarship.library.jhu.edu/server/api/core/bitstreams/fc65c319-0dbd-4a9e-9597-1c379b9bb243/content

Historicizing Black resistance in the U.S. (2024, November). American Social History Project. https://ashp.cuny.edu/historicizing-black-resistance-in-the-u-s/

History of the Federal Reserve. (n.d.). Federal Reserve Education.org. https://www.federalreserveeducation.org/about-the-fed/archive-history/

History.com Editors. (2025a, February 27). *Emancipation Proclamation*. History. https://www.history.com/articles/emancipation-proclamation

History.com Editors. (2025b, February 27). *Reconstruction*. History. https://www.history.com/articles/reconstruction

History.com Editors. (2025c, February 27). *The fireside chats*. History. https://www.history.com/topics/great-depression/fireside-chats

History.com Editors. (2025d, February 27). *The interstate highway system*. History. https://www.history.com/articles/interstate-highway-system

History.com Editors. (2025e, February 27). *Vietnamization*. History. https://www.history.com/articles/vietnamization

History.com Editors. (2025f, February 28). *Jimmy Carter*. History. https://www.history.com/articles/jimmy-carter

History.com Editors. (2025g, April 15). *Civilian Conservation Corps*. History. https://www.history.com/articles/civilian-conservation-corps

History.com Editors. (2025h, April 18). Manifest Destiny. History. https://www.history.com/articles/manifest-destiny

Hoffman, B. (2011). Health care reform and social movements in the United States. *American Journal of Public Health*, *98*(Supplement_1), S69–S79. https://doi.org/10.2105/ajph.98.supplement_1.s69

Horowitz, S. (2004). Restarting globalization after World War II: Structure, coalitions, and the Cold War. *Comparative Political Studies, 37*(2), 127–151. https://doi.org/10.1177/0010414003260980

How grassroots environmental activism has changed the course of history. (2021, September 1). Goldman Environmental Foundation. https://www.goldmanprize.org/blog/grassroots-environmental-activism/

Hunt, J. (2017). Nuclear arms control in US foreign policy. *Oxford Research Encyclopedia of American History.* https://doi.org/10.1093/acrefore/9780199329175.013.379

Iceland, J. (2015, January 6). *Did the US lose the war on poverty?* World Economic Forum. https://www.weforum.org/stories/2015/01/did-the-us-lose-the-war-on-poverty/

Indian removal. (n.d.). PBS. https://www.pbs.org/wgbh/aia/part4/4p2959.html

Indian Treaties and the Removal Act of 1830. (n.d.). Office of the Historian; United States Department of State. https://history.state.gov/milestones/1830-1860/indian-treaties

James Madison. (n.d.). American Battlefield Trust. https://www.battlefields.org/learn/biographies/james-madison

Jura, A. (2023, November 21). *Presidential Reconstruction—History, Johnson and Lincoln's plans.* Study.com. https://study.com/learn/lesson/president-andrew-johnson--lincoln-reconstruction-plan.html

Kazin, M. (2020, December 22). *Wilsonian progressivism*. Bill of Rights Institute. https://billofrightsinstitute.org/essays/wilsonian-progressivism

Kennedy, L. (2025, April 15). *What led to desegregation busing—and did it work?* History. https://www.history.com/articles/desegregation-busing-schools

Kenton, W. (2024, April 4). *Securities Act of 1933: Significance and history*. Investopedia. https://www.investopedia.com/terms/s/securitiesact1933.asp

Key speeches and writings of Gerald R. Ford. (2024, July). Gerald R. Ford Presidential Library & Museum. https://www.fordlibrarymuseum.gov/the-fords/gerald-r-ford/key-speeches-and-writings-gerald-r-ford

Kimball, D. G. (2004, July 1). *Looking back: The nuclear arms control legacy of Ronald Reagan*. Arms Control Association. https://www.armscontrol.org/act/2004-07/arms-control-today/looking-back-nuclear-arms-control-legacy-ronald-reagan

KiwiPie2859. (2022). *History*. Quizlet. https://quizlet.com/576608519/history-flash-cards/

Knott, S. (2025, January 30). *George H. W. Bush: Foreign affairs*. Miller Center. https://millercenter.org/president/bush/foreign-affairs

Kolasky, W. (2011). The election of 1912: A pivotal moment in antitrust history. *Antitrust, 25*(3), 82–88. The American Bar Association.

Korzi, M. J. (2003, June 1). *Our chief magistrate and his powers: A reconsideration of William Howard Taft's "Whig" theory of presidential leadership*. The Free Library; Farlex. https://www.thefreelibrary.com/Our+chief+magistrate+and+his+powers%3a+a+reconsideration+of+Willia m...-a0102907128

Korzi, M. J. (2021). *Presidential leadership at the crossroads*. Texas A&M University Press. https://muse.jhu.edu/book/99014

Kumar, R. (2024, December 10). *Key facts about Greta Thunberg's climate activism*. SurfsTribe. https://surfstribe.com/articles/greta-thunberg-key-facts-activism/

Lapsley, A. & Vandier, P. (2025, March 31). *Why NATO's Defence Planning Process will transform the Alliance for decades to come*. Atlantic Council. https://www.atlanticcouncil.org/in-depth-research-reports/issue-brief/why-natos-defence-planning-process-will-transform-the-alliance-for-decades-to-come/

Latham, A. (2025, March 5). *Donald Trump's America First plan: Less war, more economic nationalism*. 19FortyFive. https://www.19fortyfive.com/2025/03/donald-trumps-america-first-plan-less-war-more-economic-nationalism/

Lee, C. A. (2024). Polarization, casualty sensitivity, and military operations: Evidence from a survey experiment. *Polarization and US Foreign Policy*, 347–372. https://doi.org/10.1007/978-3-031-58618-7_12

Leffler, M. P. (2018). Ronald Reagan and the Cold War: What mattered most. *Texas National Security Review*, *1*(3), 76–89. https://doi.org/10.15781/T2FJ29W93

Leibiger, S. (2020, December 22). *The Alien and Sedition Acts*. Bill of Rights Institute. https://billofrightsinstitute.org/essays/the-alien-and-sedition-acts

Levering, R. (2019, November 12). *How anti-Vietnam War protests thwarted Nixon's plans and saved lives*. Waging Nonviolence. https://wagingnonviolence.org/2019/11/anti-vietnam-war-moratorium-mobilization-nixon/

Levinson-Waldman, R. & Panduranga, H. (2021, September 15). *Invasive and ineffective: DHS surveillance since 9/11*. Brennan Center for Justice. https://www.brennancenter.org/our-work/analysis-opinion/invasive-and-ineffective-dhs-surveillance-911

Lewis, J. (2020, October 21). *The Louisiana Purchase: Jefferson's noble bargain?* Internet Archive. https://archive.org/details/louisianapurchas0000lewi/mode/2up

Li, Z. (2024). From "Americanization" to "Vietnamization": Johnson's and Nixon's Vietnam War Policies (1963–1972). *Advances in Social Science, Education and Humanities Research*, 700–716. https://doi.org/10.2991/978-2-38476-323-8_81

Lincoln's second inaugural address. (2022). Course Hero. https://www.coursehero.com/lit/Lincolns-Second-Inaugural-Address/quotes/

Liu, Z. (2022). On the role of social media in the presidential campaign. *International Journal of Education and Humanities*, *3*(2), 53–55.

The Louisiana Purchase. (n.d.). Monticello. https://www.monticello.org/thomas-jefferson/louisiana-lewis-clark/the-louisiana-purchase/

Madison's presidency and the war of 1812: Challenges and achievements. (2024, August 13). U.S. Presidents. https://presidents.website/madisons-presidency-and-the-war-of-1812-challenges-and-achievements/

Mann, B. (2023). *Carter makes human rights a central theme of foreign policy.* EBSCO Information Services. https://www.ebsco.com/research-starters/history/carter-makes-human-rights-central-theme-foreign-policy

Martinez, R. (2023, August 3). *10 key moments from the conservative revolution of the 1980s.* The Political Insider. https://thepoliticalinsider.com/10-key-moments-from-the-conservative-revolution-of-the-1980s/

Maurantonio, N. (2014). The politics of memory. *The Oxford Handbook of Political Communication.* https://doi.org/10.1093/oxfordhb/9780199793471.013.026

McClung, C. (n.d.). *Roosevelt and the Square Deal.* United States History II; Lumen. https://courses.lumenlearning.com/wm-ushistory2/chapter/roosevelt-and-the-square-deal/

McNamara, R. (2020, November 4). *American Indian Removal Policy and the Trail of Tears.* ThoughtCo. https://www.thoughtco.com/the-trail-of-tears-1773597

The Modern Civil Rights Movement and the Kennedy administration. (2022, February 28). The John F. Kennedy Presidential Library and Museum. https://www.jfklibrary.org/learn/about-jfk/jfk-in-history/civil-rights-movement

Monroe Doctrine, 1823. (n.d.). Office of the Historian. https://history.state.gov/milestones/1801-1829/monroe

The Monroe Doctrine: A legacy of influence and controversy. (2022, October 19). US History. https://ushistory.online/monroe-doctrine/

Monten, J. (2005). The roots of the Bush doctrine: Power, nationalism, and democracy promotion in U.S. strategy. *International Security, 29*(4), 112–156. https://www.jstor.org/stable/4137499

Moran, J. (2023, March 21). *Nixon and the Pentagon Papers.* Miller Center. https://millercenter.org/the-presidency/educational-resources/first-domino-nixon-and-the-pentagon-papers

Mosher, F. C. (1985). Presidential transitions and foreign policy: The American experience. *Public Administration Review, 45*(4), 468. https://doi.org/10.2307/3110030

Murphy, C. (2008). The evolution of the modern rhetorical presidency: A critical response. *Presidential Studies Quarterly, 38*(2), 300–307. https://doi.org/10.2307/41219674

NCC Staff. (2020, November 5). *FDR's third-term election and the 22nd Amendment.* National Constitution Center. https://constitutioncenter.org/blog/fdrs-third-term-decision-and-the-22nd-amendment

NCC Staff. (2023, October 20). *The Louisiana Purchase: Jefferson's constitutional gamble*. National Constitution Center. https://constitutioncenter.org/blog/the-louisiana-purchase-jeffersons-constitutional-gamble

Nisbett, N. & Spaiser, V. (2023). Moral power of youth activists—Transforming international climate politics? *Global Environmental Change-Human and Policy Dimensions, 82*, 102717–102717. https://doi.org/10.1016/j.gloenvcha.2023.102717

Nittle, N. K. (2021, March 11). *President Jimmy Carter's record on civil rights and race relations*. ThoughtCo. https://www.thoughtco.com/president-jimmy-carters-civil-rights-record-2834612

Nixon's record on Civil Rights. (2022, April 8). Richard Nixon Foundation. https://www.nixonfoundation.org/2017/08/nixons-record-civil-rights-2/

O'Malley, F. (n.d.). Mock ratification debates: Louisiana Purchase. In *Teach Us History*. http://www1.udel.edu/teachushistory/resources/middle/jefferson/louisiana_purchase.pdf

Origins of the modern American presidency. (2020, August 18). Miller Center. https://millercenter.org/the-presidency/teacher-resources/recasting-presidential-history/origins-modern-american-presidency

Osmani, A. (2015). *Abraham Lincoln and emancipation*. Library of Congress. https://www.loc.gov/collections/abraham-lincoln-papers/articles-and-essays/abraham-lincoln-and-emancipation/

Ostler, J. (2024). *Trails of Tears, Plural: What we don't know about Indian Removal*. The National Endowment for the Humanities. https://www.neh.gov/article/trails-tears-plural-what-we-dont-know-about-indian-removal

Ostovar, M. (2024, January 16). *The decision to go to the Moon: President John F. Kennedy's May 25, 1961 speech before a joint session of Congress*. NASA. https://www.nasa.gov/history/the-decision-to-go-to-the-moon/

Palmadessa, A. L. (2023). Presidential directives and Congressional negotiations: The Higher Education Act of 1965. *Power, Discourse, and the Purpose of Policy in Higher Education*, 31–50. https://doi.org/10.1007/978-3-031-43706-9_3

Parmenter, J. (2020). Indigenous Nations and US Foreign Relations. *Oxford Research Encyclopedia of American History*. https://doi.org/10.1093/acrefore/9780199329175.013.744

Peace Corps. (2024, November 7). John F. Kennedy Presidential Library and Museum. https://www.jfklibrary.org/learn/about-jfk/jfk-in-history/peace-corps

Peterson, E. (2019, July 17). *Presidential power surges*. Harvard Law Today. https://hls.harvard.edu/today/presidential-power-surges/

Posner, M. (2025, January 6). *Jimmy Carter's enduring legacy on human rights*. Forbes. https://www.forbes.com/sites/michaelposner/2025/01/06/jimmy-carters-enduring-legacy-on-human-rights/

Prasch, A. M. (2011). *A rhetorical analysis of Franklin D. Roosevelt's pre-war "fireside chats."* https://conservancy.umn.edu/server/api/core/bitstreams/e70e3ddc-fb9e-4a19-8b72-73d37e46456d/content

The presidency of James Madison. (2023, October 25). SOCIALSTUDIESHELP.COM. https://socialstudieshelp.com/american-history-lessons/madison-war-of-1812/

President Nixon's speech on "Vietnamization," November 3, 1969. (2025, March 6). Vassar. https://www.vassar.edu/the-wars-for-vietnam/documents/president-nixons-speech-vietnamization-november-3-1969

Pruitt, S. (2025, January 31). *George Washington warned against political infighting in his farewell address.* History. https://www.history.com/articles/george-washington-farewell-address-warnings

Ragosta, J. (2018, April 16). *Thomas Jefferson and religious freedom.* Monticello. https://www.monticello.org/research-education/thomas-jefferson-encyclopedia/thomas-jefferson-and-religious-freedom/

The Reagan presidency. (n.d.). Ronald Reagan Presidential Library and Museum; National Archives. https://www.reaganlibrary.gov/reagans/reagan-administration/reagan-presidency

Reeder, T. (2024, December 3). *James Madison: Impact and legacy.* Miller Center. https://millercenter.org/president/madison/impact-and-legacy

Richardson, G. (2013, November 22). *The Great Depression.* Federal Reserve History. https://www.federalreservehistory.org/essays/great-depression?ref=brandon-giella

Richmond, Y. (2014, February). *Helsinki and human rights.* American Diplomacy. https://americandiplomacy.web.unc.edu/2014/02/helsinki-and-human-rights/

Riley, R. (2023, August 28). *Bill Clinton: Foreign affairs.* Miller Center. https://millercenter.org/president/clinton/foreign-affairs

Rogers Stevens, C., Estes, T., McDonald, C. & Eicholz, H. (2025, March 20). *Jefferson in time: Perspectives through his eyes.* The Online Library of Liberty. https://oll.libertyfund.org/publications/liberty-matters/2025-03-20-jefferson-in-time-perspectives-through-his-eyes#post_1716

Rottinghaus, B. (2006). Rethinking presidential responsiveness: The public presidency and rhetorical congruency, 1953–2001. *The Journal of Politics, 68*(3), 720–732. https://doi.org/10.1111/j.1468-2508.2006.00457.x

Rowland, R. & Jones, J. (2016). Reagan's strategy for the Cold War and the Evil Empire address. *Rhetoric and Public Affairs, 19*(3), 427–464. https://doi.org/10.14321/rhetpublaffa.19.3.0427

Rust, R. (2025a, February 26). *The Great Depression and the New Deal.* American History Central. https://www.americanhistorycentral.com/entries/progressive-era-great-depression-and-new-deal/

Rust, R. (2025b, February 26). *Woodrow Wilson and progressivism.* American History Central. https://www.americanhistorycentral.com/entries/progressive-era-woodrow-wilson-and-progressivism/

Sanches, D. (2013, November 22). The second World War and its aftermath. Federal Reserve History. https://www.federalreservehistory.org/essays/wwii-and-its-aftermath

Sarotte, M. E. (2019). How to enlarge NATO: The debate inside the Clinton administration, 1993–95. *International Security, 44*(1), 7–41. https://doi.org/10.1162/isec_a_00353

Schmitz, D. F. & Walker, V. (2004). Jimmy Carter and the foreign policy of human rights: The development of a post-Cold War foreign policy. *Diplomatic History, 28*(1), 113–143. https://www.jstor.org/stable/24914773

Searles, H. (2024, March 24). *Peace Democrats (Copperheads).* American History Central. https://www.americanhistorycentral.com/entries/peace-democrats-aka-copperheads/

Selverstone, M. (2023, October 8). *JFK and the Cuban Missile Crisis.* Miller Center. https://millercenter.org/the-presidency/educational-resources/jfk-and-cuban-missile-crisis

Sherwin, M. J. (2020, October 16). *Inside JFK's decision-making during the Cuban Missile Crisis.* Time. https://time.com/5899754/jfk-decisionmaking-cuban-missile-crisis/

Shongwe, V. (2025, April 3). *How Trump's tariffs reshape US trade policy in a globalised economy*. IOL. https://www.iol.co.za/sundayindependent/dispatch/how-trumps-tariffs-reshape-us-trade-policy-in-a-globalised-economy-43710b08-78f3-47d5-a8bc-4a71eee68d8f

Shvangiradze, T. (2025, March 24). *5 events that characterized Cold War détente*. The Collector. https://www.thecollector.com/events-characterized-cold-war-detente/

Sinnar, S. (2022, April). *Hate crimes, terrorism, and the framing of white supremacist violence*. California Law Review. https://www.californialawreview.org/print/hate-crimes-terrorism-and-the-framing-of-white-supremacist-violence

Smink, T. W. A. (2022). *The American push for NATO enlargement 1989-1999*. In *DSpace*. https://theses.ubn.ru.nl/bitstreams/554196df-5f98-4c59-a428-67eec1f36d49/download

Søndergaard, R. S. (2015). Bill Clinton's "Democratic Enlargement" and the securitisation of democracy promotion. *Diplomacy & Statecraft*, *26*(3), 534–551. https://doi.org/10.1080/09592296.2015.1067529

Sonnenfeld, J. A. (2025, January 2). *How Jimmy Carter lost his job and found his mission: A personal remembrance*. Yale Insights. https://insights.som.yale.edu/insights/how-jimmy-carter-lost-his-job-and-found-his-mission-personal-remembrance

Special message to the Congress on equal educational opportunities and school busing. (n.d.). The American Presidency Project. https://www.presidency.ucsb.edu/documents/special-message-the-congress-equal-educational-opportunities-and-school-busing

Stockwell, M. (n.d.). *Presidential precedents*. George Washington's Mount Vernon. https://www.mountvernon.org/library/digitalhistory/digital-encyclopedia/article/presidential-precedents

Strong, R. (2025, January 31). *Jimmy Carter: Domestic affairs*. Miller Center. https://millercenter.org/president/carter/domestic-affairs

Suciu, P. (2024, February 19). Presidents and their relationship with media—it's been complicated. *Forbes*. https://www.forbes.com/sites/petersuciu/2024/02/19/presidents-and-their-relationship-with-media-its-been-complicated/

Sun, C., Perner, S. & Chen, X. (2025, March 17). *The political logic of the resurgence of Trumpism and its impact on US foreign policy by SHI Zehua*. ChinAffairs+. https://www.chinaffairsplus.com/p/the-political-logic-of-the-resurgence

Swanson, W. (2022, May 20). *The Keynote Address: On unity and equality*. Lincoln Group of the District of Columbia. https://www.lincolnian.org/post/the-keynote-address-on-unity-and-equality

Terrell, E. (2025, February 28). *National Recovery Administration (NRA) and the New Deal: A resource guide*. Library of Congress. https://guides.loc.gov/national-recovery-administration

Theodore Roosevelt. (2024, March 29). New York State. https://empirestateplaza.ny.gov/hall-governors/theodore-roosevelt

Thomas Jefferson and the Virginia Statute for Religious Freedom. (n.d.). Virginia Museum of History & Culture. https://virginiahistory.org/learn/thomas-jefferson-and-virginia-statute-religious-freedom

Tower, C. (1914). The European attitude toward the Monroe Doctrine. *Proceedings of the American Society of International Law at Its Annual Meeting (1907-1917)*, *8*, 202–217. JSTOR. https://doi.org/10.2307/25656503

Trump's trade war is no bluff. (2025, April 20). MENAFN. https://menafn.com/1109449548/Trumps-trade-war-is-no-bluff

The Trust Buster. (n.d.). U.S. History. https://www.ushistory.org/us/43b.asp

Tsim, E. (2025, April 24). *Trump can endure trade war with China*. The Daily Targum. https://dailytargum.com/article/tsim-trump-can-endure-trade-war-with-china-20250424

Tucker, D. (2024, July 1). *Speech on the constitutionality of the Louisiana Purchase*. Teaching American History. https://teachingamericanhistory.org/document/speech-on-the-constitutionality-of-the-louisiana-purchase/

The 2020–21 presidential transition. (2022, January 20). Center for Presidential Transition. https://presidentialtransition.org/reports-publications/2020-21-lessons-learned/

Tyszkiewicz, J. (2022). Human rights and the Jimmy Carter administration's policy towards Poland, 1977–80. *Cold War History*, *23*(2), 307–325. https://doi.org/10.1080/14682745.2022.2102606

United in remembrance, divided over policies. (2011, September 1). Pew Research Center. https://www.pewresearch.org/politics/2011/09/01/united-in-remembrance-divided-over-policies/

Varon, E. R. (2016). Andrew Johnson and the legacy of the Civil War. *Oxford Research Encyclopedia of American History*. https://doi.org/10.1093/acrefore/9780199329175.013.11

Varon, E. R. (2023, August 28). *Andrew Johnson: Impact and legacy*. Miller Center. https://millercenter.org/president/johnson/impact-and-legacy

Volle, A. (2024). Reaganomics. In *Britannica*. https://www.britannica.com/topic/Reaganomics

Vorberg, L. & Zeitler, A. (2019). "This is (not) entertainment!": Media constructions of political scandal discourses in the 2016 US presidential election. *Media, Culture & Society*, *41*(4), 417–432. https://doi.org/10.1177/0163443719833288

Wall, W. L. (2016). The New Deal. *Oxford Research Encyclopedia of American History*. https://doi.org/10.1093/acrefore/9780199329175.013.87

Washington, G. (1796, September 19). *Farewell address.* Center for Political Thought and Leadership; Arizona State University.
https://civics.asu.edu/sites/default/files/2021-06/Q86%20Washington%2C%20Farewell%20Address%20%281796%29_CPTL.pdf

Webb, R., Kurtz, L. & Rosenthal, S. (2020). *When politics trump science: The erosion of science-based regulation.* Environmental Law Institute.
https://climate.law.columbia.edu/sites/climate.law.columbia.edu/files/content/Webb%20et%20al.%20--%20When%20Politics%20Trump%20Science%20--%20Sept.%202020.pdf

Weingroff, R. F. (2017, June 27). *The greatest decade 1956–1966.* Highway History; Federal Highway Administration.
https://www.fhwa.dot.gov/infrastructure/50interstate2.cfm

Wheelock, D. C. (2021, September 13). *Overview: The history of the Federal Reserve.* Federal Reserve History.
https://www.federalreservehistory.org/essays/federal-reserve-history

Wile, R. & Murphy, J. (2025, March 14). *Tariff timeline: How Trump turned global trade into an economic battlefield.* NBC News.
https://www.nbcnews.com/business/economy/tariff-timeline-trump-trade-war-global-economy-rcna196487

Wilmoth Lerner, A. (2025, March 27). *"Mr. Carmody, we want lights": The Tennessee Valley Authority and rural electrification under the New Deal.* Encyclopedia.com. https://www.encyclopedia.com/science/encyclopedias-almanacs-transcripts-and-maps/mr-carmody-we-want-lights-tennessee-valley-authority-and-rural-electrification-under-new-deal

With malice toward none: The Abraham Lincoln Bicentennial Exhibition. (2009, February 12). Library of Congress. https://www.loc.gov/exhibits/lincoln/lincoln-as-commander-in-chief.html

Woerner, J. (2023, November 21). *Trust busting—definition, president and progressive era.* Study.com. https://study.com/academy/lesson/trust-busting-and-government-regulations-on-economy-industry-in-the-progressive-era.html

Zielinski, A. E. (2024, July 19). *The first American president: Setting the precedent.* American Battlefield Trust. https://www.battlefields.org/learn/articles/first-american-president-setting-precedent

www.ingramcontent.com/pod-product-compliance
Lightning Source LLC
Chambersburg PA
CBHW050246010526
44107CB00003B/204